D0187709

Praise for *7 Strategies for Developing Capable Students*

"These strategies offer a clear set of principles and guidelines to help parents and teachers deal with the struggles, challenges, joys, and discoveries children face as they prepare for their future. I highly recommend this book to all parents and educators."
> —**Robert W. Reasoner, president,**
> **International Council for Self-Esteem**

"What makes *7 Strategies for Developing Capable Students* so powerful is its focus on what parents can do at home in order to help children become responsible students and young adults. This book is a must-read for parents!"
> —**Bruce F. Colston, Ed.D., consultant and trainer**

"This book is both relevant and compelling."
> —**Kelly F. Blanton, superintendent of schools,**
> **Kern County, California**

"With an emphasis on prevention, this book joins H. Stephen Glenn's first book, *Raising Self-Reliant Children in a Self-Indulgent World,* as a must for every parent's library."
> —**Phyl R. Brinkley, M.Ed.**

"What have you learned, Dorothy?"
"Well . . . I think that it wasn't enough just to want to see Uncle Henry and Auntie Em. And that if I ever go looking for my heart's desire again, I won't look any further than my own back-yard, because if it isn't there, I never really lost it to begin with . . . Because there's no place like home, there's no place like home, there's no place like home . . ."

—The Wizard of Oz

▼

7 Strategies
for Developing
Capable* Students

*responsible, respectful, and resourceful

H. Stephen Glenn, Ph.D.
Michael L. Brock, M.A.

Prima Publishing

PRIMA PUBLISHING and colophon are registered trademarks of Prima Communications, Inc.

Library of Congress Cataloging-in-Publication Data

Glenn, H. Stephen
    7 strategies for developing capable students / H. Stephen Glenn and Michael L. Brock.
        p.   cm.
    Includes index.
    ISBN 0-7615-1356-6
    1. Home and school—United States.   2. Education—Parent participation—United States.   3. Parent and child—United States.
    4. Child development—United States.   I. Brock, Michael L.
    II. Title.
    LC225.3.G54   1998
    370.19'2—dc21   98-11153
                                                                      CIP

98 99 00 01 HH 10 9 8 7 6 5 4 3
Printed in the United States of America

How to Order
Single copies may be ordered from Prima Publishing, P.O. Box 1260BK, Rocklin, CA 95677; telephone (916) 632-4400. Quantity discounts are also available. On your letterhead, include information concerning the intended use of the books and the number of books you wish to purchase.

Visit us online at www.primapublishing.com

For hundreds of parents, teachers, and DCP (Developing Capable People) course leaders who have shared their struggles and celebrations, and most of all for Judy Arleen, our seven children—Jennifer, Keri, John, Kristi, Becky, Kimbi, and Michael—and now nine grandchildren for whom these principles will make a great difference.

—*H. Stephen Glenn, Ph.D.*

This work is dedicated to Carol, my wife and best friend, and to Thomas and Jennifer, our grown-up children. May they forgive me for the stories I have told about them.

—*Michael L. Brock, M.A.*

▼

Contents

▼

Foreword

How does your garden grow? Flowers bloom in a nurturing environment where they receive the proper amounts of water and sunlight or shade to reach their individual, full potential—and their individual, full potential is all we expect. We don't expect a petunia to become a rose, but only the best petunia it can be. What happens when flowers don't receive the proper amounts of sunlight and water? Obviously they don't develop fully . . . or they die. To prevent this, a gardener learns how much water and sunlight or shade each flower needs and provides it accordingly.

How do your children grow? Children bloom in a nurturing environment where they receive the proper amounts of love and guidance to reach their individual, full potential. As adults, we don't always give children the respect we give to flowers. We don't always take the time to educate ourselves on exactly what our children need to reach their individual, full potential. Sometimes we expect children to fit a mold in the area of academic achievement—we want all roses instead of a variety of flowers—which can be very discouraging to children and may result in resistance and rebellion instead of achievement.

As parents, we don't mean to discourage our children, and more often than not we don't realize we are creating discouragement within them. Many common mistakes we make are made in the name of love, including:

- Conveying to children that their achievement in school is more important to us than they themselves are, thereby communicating that our love for them is conditional.

- Failing to model the spirit of cooperation at home through shared household chores and responsibilities, thereby placing barriers before children's contributions to the various communities (for example, school) that they will find themselves in.

- Engaging in power struggles, thereby preventing children from experiencing the natural consequences of their choices and from developing the personal responsibility learned from those experiences and consequences.

- Doing too much for children (for example, doing their homework for them), thereby communicating that they are not capable of handling the many responsibilities that life gives them.

- Failing to provide experiences that help children feel capable and that help develop the life skills of self-discipline, responsibility, and problem-solving.

This book is about providing a nurturing environment that is essential for children's success and happiness in school, as well as in all phases of life. It provides the education parents need to help their children develop to their maximum potential. It teaches parents:

- How to help children feel capable of doing things for themselves, thereby empowering them to handle their school responsibilities with confidence and effectiveness.

- How to help children feel unconditionally loved and experience belonging and significance, thereby allowing them to start school each morning knowing that who they are is not determined by their level of achievement.

- How to avoid power struggles, thereby modeling cooperation and problem solving (critical skills for success and happiness in school).

- How to inspire self-motivation in children, thereby helping them become self-directed learners for life.

- How to strive for an emotionally stable home environment, thereby providing the oasis that children need when things at school don't go as well as they would like.

- How to provide the experiences that help children feel capable and help them develop the life skills of self-discipline, responsibility, and problem-solving, thereby laying the groundwork for a happy and successful school experience.

In this book, you will find the encouragement and tools to provide fertile soil for your children to grow into capable students and capable human beings. Providing encouragement will allow children to see themselves as capable, significant young people who can make choices that actively influence the direction of their lives; and providing tools helps them positively influence their education by developing responsibility, self-discipline, communication skills, and the ability to make effective and ethical choices. Our children are deserving of nothing less than this.

—Jane Nelsen, Ed.D., M.F.C.C.
author of the bestselling
POSITIVE DISCIPLINE series

Introduction

April Is the Cruelest Month

April is the cruelest month, breeding
Lilacs out of the dead land, mixing
Memory and desire, stirring
Dull roots with spring rain.

—T. S. Eliot, *The Waste Land*

Thomas Stearns Eliot, the great American-born British poet, must have been reflecting on his teaching days when he wrote those opening lines to *The Waste Land*. April is indeed a cruel month: Ask any teacher. There are still two months or so before the school year comes to a close, spring fever has awakened any still-dormant hormones, and students are moving quickly toward "summer vacation."

The grass on the playground is beaten and dull. Spring rains soak the soil, keeping children indoors.

Students find their need for outdoor recess frustrated, their memories overloaded, their desires focused mostly on summer. Who can blame them after the long journey out of winter?

Teachers also feel the pull of summertime. The school year seems to stretch endlessly in both directions. It has been a long year of grading papers, implementing a curriculum that may or may not meet student needs, and working to support the efforts of parents and their children.

It has been an incredibly challenging year of working with students who come from widely diverse backgrounds with needs ranging from essential learning skills to even more basic social and life skills. Each day has brought an increasing struggle to reach students already saturated—via technology such as TV, video games, and the Internet—with wonders and concerns unimaginable just a generation ago. All this, plus the pressure of managing their own families on salaries that are a national embarrassment, has just about drained the well!

Yes, April is the cruelest month. For reasons not entirely clear (though certainly related to the factors noted above), there is something about the springtime, particularly April, that dislocates families. Such upset results in a sharp upward rise in the stress curve that settles only when summer brings welcome respite. (At least life settles down for educators . . . parents may have very different perspectives on the summer!)

Michael's Journey

For all my years in the "real world" of work, I have been an educator. I've spent more than twenty of those years as an elementary school principal. I don't know what the word "principal" conjures up for you—whether it brings forth pleasant or not-so-pleasant memories—but your perception does matter because it colors your expectations of what your children will be experiencing in school.

The Principal's Office

Parents often refer to being "sent to the principal's office," suggesting experiences they would rather forget. I hope that is not your experience! More importantly, I hope that is not your child's experience!

Today, more than ever before, the principal's office (and every teacher's classroom) needs to be a place of comfort for our children, a place where they gain opportunities for contribution, feel a sense of affirmation, and experience an environment characterized by emotional stability. Principals' offices and classrooms should not be places children are "sent," but places to which they are invited and welcomed.

The noun "principal" derives from its adjective form: I am the *principal* (that is, the *main, chief,* or *head*) teacher of the school. As the head teacher of the school, I am called upon to be a **role model,** not only for my teaching abilities, but for my enthusiasm, optimism, and positive expectations as well. Mostly, I am called upon to be a role model of positive expectations.

Seven Days in April

It was a seven-day period in April of 1991 that started the chain of events that changed the direction of my life. I shifted from my primary role as a child educator to the role of parent educator. I resisted at first, since I chose this business to help *children* . . . not their parents! . . . But since I took my first tentative steps, my new role has been filled with wonders, challenges, and remarkable changes.

The experience began with a series of incidents that challenged my ability to enthusiastically project positive expectations, and I felt myself descending into uncharacteristic pessimism. I'd always tried to live (or at least preach!) the old adage that "inconveniences are adventures wrongly considered." Suddenly I found myself questioning whether some of the "adventures" coming my way were worth the inconvenience.

Maria It all started rather uneventfully. A parent had dropped by to tell me that she was leaving her husband of ten years due to continuing emotional abuse. The stress, she said, was proving too much for her third-grade daughter. She then asked if I would take time throughout the day to check on Maria to make sure she was handling it okay. This was not an unusual situation; in fact, I've become much accustomed to it through the years, as divorce continues to affect more and more American families. Statisticians estimate that about one out of three (predictions go as high as fifty-fifty!) marriages that took place in 1990 will end in divorce.

Richard I had just returned to my office after checking on Maria when another mom stopped by. Her husband of twenty years had recently walked out, leaving her with six children and a part-time job. She told me that Richard, her sixteen-year-old who had graduated from our school, was taking the divorce harder than the others and had run away from home. She knew we encourage our graduates to stop by whenever they wish, and many do, often just to talk. If Richard should come by the school, she asked, would I tell him that she was worried and ask him to please call home?

Teddy A few days later, two of our middle school teachers visited me. By necessity, all middle school teachers are counselors, whether formally trained or not. Students in the middle school grades (grades six through eight, encompassing ages 11–15 in most schools) demand a very special kind of teacher—one who is firm yet approachable, thick-skinned yet deeply sensitive, open-minded yet firmly principle-centered. Middle-school teachers must, above all, be good listeners . . . and steadfastly resist the temptation to sermonize.

These two teachers, the leaders of our middle school, came with a concern. A seventh-grade boy would not leave one of his female classmates alone. He insisted on writing her suggestive notes, calling her at home, following her around throughout the day, jockeying for a position to sit next to her at every opportunity. Before long he was making unwelcome physical contact.

The girl continued to make it clear that his advances were neither welcome nor appropriate, as did the teachers. Still, his inappropriate behavior continued and, in fact, was escalating. They feared his obsession was more than just teenage infatuation, and that it could easily lead to much worse. "Harassment" was not too strong a word; "stalking" also described what was happening.

Would I speak with the boy "man to man," they wondered? Should we invite the parents in and urge counseling—for both the boy and his parents? If necessary, could we temporarily remove the boy from the school to protect the girl?

I chose the less extreme approach and set up a conference with the boy, fumbling through the conversation with my amateur counseling techniques. I became increasingly aware that just as our parents needed help in parenting, I needed help with "principaling."

Two days later, the same teachers visited again, I assumed to update me on Teddy, the seventh-grader who wouldn't leave the girl of his dreams alone. But another problem had developed.

Joanna   Fourteen-year-old Joanna had brought a one-hundred-dollar bill to school, and the money was stolen from her. The teachers were concerned, of course, that classmates were stealing from each other, but were even more concerned about what Joanna was doing with a hundred-dollar bill at school . . . and about where she got the money.

We spent the rest of the school year dealing with the problem of Joanna and her stolen money. We found out who took it—two of Joanna's girlfriends who had grown tired of her coming to school with large sums of money and flaunting it in front of everyone. But that was hardly the end of the matter. The taking of the money turned out to be our lesser concern, once we discovered that Joanna had regularly come to school with large sums of money all year long. Where was she getting it?

Unfortunately, we never solved that mystery. Joanna's parents refused to acknowledge the problem and would not respond to our efforts to provide counseling. The school year ran out, and Joanna graduated with her secret. In subsequent years, we put together bits and pieces of the mystery, and the more we learned, the more it became evident that the source of the money was, in fact, a result of our worst fears: drug involvement.

The Abused Ones

Scattered during those same seven April days were three calls to my office regarding possible parental abuse of students in our school. Working with child welfare personnel was nothing new for me in my role as school principal, but three abuse calls in seven days was a record.

Three calls concerning abuse, a mom leaving her husband and concerned about her third-grader, another mom looking for her runaway son, a seventh-grader stalking another student, a theft of $100 (and the greater issue of how a fourteen-year-old girl regularly got such large sums of money)—all this within seven days in the sheltered environment of a small, highly acclaimed, suburban elementary school in the Dallas, Texas, area!

Each situation contained a common element—a family problem resulting in a student problem. Maria, the little third-grader, was having difficulty at school because her mom had just left her husband. Richard, the sixteen-year-old, had run away from home because he couldn't handle his father's desertion of his mom. Teddy couldn't deal with his attraction to the young girl because he lacked role models for appropriate display of affection at home—his parents' relationship was characterized by almost continuous hostility and aggressiveness, both verbal and physical.

Joanna was raised in a home with parents who held nothing but the highest expectations for their children's success, accepting no excuses for their being less than number one in all endeavors. Realizing early on that she could not be first in any accepted avenue of student achievement (her older sister had claimed that star in the family constellation), Joanna looked for other avenues to prove herself. Unfortunately, her confused attempts to attain personal significance came through crime.

All three abuse cases were directly parent-related as well. Seven students within a week seriously suffered at school because of problems at home and a lack of resources to enable them to deal effectively with these unpleasant home situations. Perhaps I needed a different approach to identifying and meeting the needs of the students. Or even better, perhaps I needed to place the challenge of helping our students in a broader perspective—one that approached students within the context of an interconnected system consisting of Mom, Dad, brothers, and sisters; a system in which each member's hopes, joys, pain, and struggles affect (and are affected by) all other members—a system called the family.

An Alternative

Sometime during those seven days I was introduced to the world of parent support in the form of a brochure that crossed my desk—an invitation to attend the **Developing Capable People** Leadership Training Workshop, designed and led by H. Stephen Glenn. Skimming the brochure, I read that by attending the workshop I could learn ways to help reduce family conflicts, encourage the development of healthy self-concept in young people, and provide opportunities for both young people and their families to increase their resources for dealing with the challenges of life.

I read that we would look at families in transition and learn how to help young people develop the perceptions of their own capability, significance, and influence over their environment, as well as skills in self-discipline, communication, responsibility, and judgment. I learned that my participation in the workshop would certify me to lead a nine-week series of classes designed to help adults who work with children and youth learn how to develop these perceptions and skills.

I mumbled something to the effect that I needed this workshop about a year ago, not now; but going on the old maxim that it's never too late, I signed up for the three-day training program. If I were to stay in the profession of school principal, I clearly needed to experience what this workshop claimed to offer. If nothing else, I reasoned, it would provide three well-deserved, relaxing days away from school. For those three days at least, I could leave the problems of Maria, Richard, Teddy, and Joanna; the deserted moms; and the abused subjects of the three phone calls behind me.

By the close of the third workshop day, I was a whirl-wind of mixed emotions. More than anything, I was over-whelmed and exhausted—three relaxing days it definitely was *not!*

But I experienced something else during those days—a feeling of empowerment. Overwhelmed as I was, unsure about much of the experience, physically and mentally exhausted, I still left that workshop convinced that I had something to bring to my school parents that would answer many of the concerns we were all dealing with.

Empowered by this confidence and armed with my new toolbox of resources, I returned to school and immediately scheduled the course I had been trained to lead . . . and have been conducting these courses ever since!

My experiences during that April and the insights I have gained during my continuing involvement in Developing Capable People training and workshops have led me to reflect seriously on the relationship between parents' and teachers' perceptions and skills and children's success and happiness in school. Those seven days in April certainly presented some extreme situations for me to ponder, but those days brought all the "small" issues as well. We constantly faced the more mundane challenges that confront educators and parents every day—homework not being done, children not working up to potential, students stressed out trying to meet their own or someone else's expectations, tardiness, classroom disruptions, playground fights, too much work, too little time, and so on. . . .

Reflecting on the extreme as well as the everyday issues, I found myself asking: What parental attitudes and behaviors most encourage success and happiness in school? What practices at home allow children to arrive at school willing to learn, confident in their abilities, able to manage emotional baggage that would otherwise impede learning? What, in short, can parents do to maximize the value of a child's school experience?

Stephen's Journey

During the turbulent 1960s, I became very interested in the struggle of young people in America and began to do research and write articles on my findings. In 1969–1972, I directed one of the first demonstration projects funded by the U.S. Office of Education (USOE) under the Drug Abuse Prevention Act of 1970. This project involved training teams of parents and teachers to work effectively with young people in community and school settings.

When the USOE decided to make this approach the basis for the national program called "Help Communities Help Themselves," I became director of the Southeast Regional Training Center from 1972–1975. During this time I also served as a consultant to the Alcohol, Drug and Mental Health Administration (ADAMHA); the National Institute on Drug Abuse (NIDA); and the White House Special Action Office for Drug Abuse Prevention (SAODAP).

These activities gave me tremendous exposure to research on a broad spectrum of community, school, and family issues, as well as on program strategies involving young people. By 1976, when I was director of the National Drug Abuse Training Center, it was apparent to me that a large **"common ground"** underlay behavioral health problems manifesting themselves in many different systems.

Using staff and resources of the center, we conducted an extensive "state-of-the-art" review, which resulted in the first federal document to specifically identify three perceptions and four skills (The Significant Seven, discussed in chapter 3) as primary targets for prevention, intervention, and treatment programming (*The National Institute on Drug Abuse Manpower and Training Strategy*, HEW 1977). In the intervening twenty years, a steady accumulation of research has validated the essential reliability of this policy recommendation—for example, Search Institute, *Youth Asset Development;* Hawkins and Catalano, *Risk and Protective Factors;* Bernard, *Resiliency;* PIRE, *Social Competency and Refusal Skills;* Reasoner, *Healthy Self-esteem;* Olsen, *Family Cohesiveness*). *All* these researchers specifically identify several or all seven significant elements (The Significant Seven) as major factors in such problems as substance abuse, adolescent pregnancy and parenthood, dropping out, underachievement, and gang involvement.

Weaknesses in each characteristic are consistently correlated with behavioral health problems, high-risk behavior, dependency, ineffective living, and ineffective learning. Strengths in each characteristic are consistently correlated with behavioral health, low-risk behavior, independence, effective living, and effective learning.

Since 1977 my work has focused entirely on identifying strategies, developing methods, and creating resources and programs to develop and/or strengthen these characteristics in people. In 1982 the training program called Developing Capable People was first released; it has proven an extremely effective process for improving family relationships, parenting outcomes, educational effectiveness, and behavioral health, and for developing character, resiliency, emotional intelligence, and self-sufficiency.

My research also indicates that our global lifestyles and societies are rapidly changing. These changes, unfortunately, have also stripped away many of the experiences and traditional mechanisms that foster life resources, making the seven resources even more critical for today's young people than for those of previous generations.

Parents (and teachers) who learn how to encourage strength in The Significant Seven generally, and dimensions of the school experience in specific, make tremendous contributions to a young person's ability to live, learn, and love effectively. I have now had the enormous privilege of working with and studying thousands of parents and educators such as Michael who embraced these principles and helped children realize their potential in school. In many ways, this book is part of their testimony and legacy.

Our Perspective

7 Strategies for Developing Capable Students captures the perspective of pilgrims who have seen what can happen when we take a cold, hard look at our attitudes and values, hold them up to the light of dignity and respect, and reflect seriously upon what we see. It conveys the experiences of educators who have spent more than a quarter century working with parents and children in school settings. It contains the thoughts of leaders who have struggled to achieve collaboration and understanding among parents, teachers, students, business leaders, religious organizations, and communities in general. And, it expresses what parents have known, intimately—the struggles, challenges, joys, and discoveries of supporting children in their journeys through the school years!

It is written by parent/educators, and it is written *for* parents—of Maria, Richard, Joanna, and Teddy, yes; but even more for the parents whose children are *not* experiencing extreme difficulties but who might be undergoing the everyday challenges of motivation, organization, and achievement that all students face from time to time.

Except in a closing chapter titled "A Word to Teachers," we do not focus on what teachers can do to help students become more successful in their schooling. We are interested in what we parents can do *with or without* the support of educators.

Healthy people understand that they cannot change others; they can only change themselves. But in growing and changing ourselves, we often provide incentives and opportunities for others to grow and change also. Therefore, our focus in this book will not be on changing American education, a subject addressed at length at policy-making forums from local school boards to the federal government; it will be on equipping parents to create and maintain a healthy environment of support and challenge for their children.

The importance of this issue cannot be overstated. As much as we might prefer otherwise, we simply cannot change others directly. We cannot directly change the attitudes and behaviors of teachers who will have such a major influence on the lives of our children. Most of us can, at best, only slightly influence the direction of our local school system. And we probably can do very little to change the direction of American education, certainly not in the short run.

This can be frustrating, tempting us to fall into what could be called the *"if only" syndrome.* . . . *If only* the teacher would be more flexible. *If only* the school would change its rules. *If only* the school board would be more open to our concerns. Such reactions, though likely and quite understandable, represent **reactive thinking.** This means looking to the outside for rescue, for solutions beyond our circle of influence. The teacher, the school rules, the politics of the local school board are all largely outside our control. We may wish otherwise, but the truth is that we have little control over these external factors. Therefore, the more we focus on them, the more frustrated we become. Despite the frustration that comes from being faced with circumstances beyond our control in matters so important to us, we can also feel liberated by acknowledging what is beyond our control, then practicing the serenity principle advocated by Alcoholics Anonymous: *Lord grant me the serenity to accept the things I cannot change . . . the courage to change the things I can . . . and the wisdom to know the difference.* It can indeed be liberating!

Once we accept that external factors are largely outside our influence, we become free to focus our energies on what we can influence, namely ourselves, our family, our home environment. By focusing on the family, where we do have much influence, instead of on external factors, we will be doing the best we can to maximize the potential for our children to experience success and happiness in school.

So we will focus here not on what we want the teacher to do or the school to do, but only on what we can do, with the confidence that if *we* do our part as effectively as possible, then our children will develop the skills necessary to deal with the challenges of life and learning, including ineffective school situations.

Much in American education needs to be changed, and it is incumbent upon all of us to recognize that and take whatever opportunities present themselves to work for change. But the real changes, the truly long-lasting changes, will take place when we decide to concentrate our energies within ourselves and our families.

Three Parts

Part One, "The Capable Student," will discuss the importance of providing opportunities for our children to develop their capabilities, thereby empowering them to make the decisions and choices that will benefit them as they progress through their school years. The Seven

Strategies introduced in this section are drawn from the Developing Capable People program and the Seven Perceptions and Skills that are the program's foundation.

Part Two, "The Capable Family," explores essential principles for creating and maintaining an environment that develops capable students. This section has been drawn from our experiences in both consuming and providing educational services for many years and could be viewed as a "coaches' clinic" featuring:

- **Contribution**—creating a cooperative learning experience in the home through chores and responsibilities (with a special section on homework);
- **Affirmation**—showing real interest in a child's world, which goes beyond the usual call for parents to "get involved," instead encouraging parents to get into a child's world, demonstrate respect for uniqueness, and foster conditions that encourage the development of talents and self-worth;
- **Emotional Stability**—providing a family oasis in the home—an environment that is safe, secure, inviting, and conducive to emotional growth;
- **Modeling**—teaching through example, or "walking the talk"—a most important principle of parenting.

And **Part Three,** "The Capable Team," presents ways in which parents and teachers can team up for the sake of children. Here we will discuss how parents and teachers can support and encourage one another by helping children realize their potential to become capable, significant young people.

A Dialogue

We will occasionally use dialogue to demonstrate practical application of the principles presented. Some readers may feel the dialogues are not realistic. The critical issue, however, is that the principles become more apparent, and therefore more concrete, through the dialogue.

Look beyond the dialogue, then, to the principles that drive it. Try to envision yourself in a similar situation, then create your own dialogue based on the principles you discover and your own personal application. Make that new dialogue your own. Practice and live it, knowing that practice leads to ownership, and ownership leads to commitment.

▼

Part
___
I

The Capable Student

The Little Engine That Could summed it all up rather succinctly, yet somewhat simplistically: "I think I can . . . I think I can . . . I think I can." Succinct because there is much to be said for the effect of attitude on outcomes; simplistic because, after all, there's more to capability than just thinking it—try thinking your way to outrunning Olympic star Michael Johnson in the 200 meters.

The fact of the matter is that each of us has a range of capability, and whether or not we test the outer limits of that range depends on a number of factors, not the least of which is attitude. "I think I can" may not be all it takes, but it is an essential ingredient.

So it's very much worth our efforts, as we begin this look at developing capable students, to reflect on this issue of capability. Just what is a capable student? How does the capable student see herself? What are the skills that he will need to demonstrate as he deals with life, particularly life in school? chapter 1, "Developing the Capable Student," shows what is meant by being capable; chapter 2, "Barriers and Builders," presents the barriers that we sometimes place in the way of developing capability, as well as the builders we can use to overcome those barriers; chapter 3, "The Significant Seven," introduces The Significant Seven perceptions and skills that every young person needs to thrive in life; chapters 4 through 10, the "Developing Strong . . ." chapters, show us how to develop each of those perceptions and skills; and chapter 11, The Capable Family," reveals the most important thing we parents need to do to encourage our students' successes in school.

Chapter

I

Developing the Capable Student

I'm not very big but I'll do my best, and I think I can . . . I think I can . . . I think I can.

—The Little Engine That Could, *Watty Piper*

It was the second day of school, and parents and students were arriving at the school entrance very excited about the adventure of another school year. As a dad and his son, a little first-grader, approached within ten yards or so of the school door, the little boy turned to his dad and said: "Dad, you don't have to walk me in all the way. I know where my classroom is now. Bye."

The dad hesitated, looked at his son with an expression somewhere between confusion and hurt, then turned to the principal who was welcoming everyone. "What have I done wrong?" he seemed to be asking.

"Go on to work," the principal said. "You've got a real winner there, a very capable young person, anxious to show you that he's got everything in his little world under control, including school." The dad brightened, thanked the principal, and went on his way.

Later in the year the principal observed a mom walk her first-grader into the school building, into the classroom, and up to his desk; then he watched her unload the little boy's backpack, take out his books and pencils and line them up in the order he would need them; help him into his seat; kiss him good-bye between tears; and then, very reluctantly, leave.

The mother is doing all this out of love—to ensure that her son's school experience will be free from the slightest possible inconvenience. She does this because she thinks it is her job to protect him from distress, or she may also do it because she feels guilt for some real or imagined transgression, or has inherited some baggage from the past.

The Message

But what is the mother who helps so much teaching her child? What messages does her child receive from her over-attentiveness? What does he see in the mirror of her eyes?

To the objective observer, the messages to the child say that he is not a capable person, that he cannot handle the simple task of unloading his backpack, that he cannot be expected to know how to arrange the materials he will need for the day, that he cannot even find his own way to his desk.

A "No-Win" Triangle

The negative effects of his mother's rescuing and enabling are apparent to the boy's teacher, who reports that his response to challenges is far more often "I can't" than

"I can." The boy's lack of confidence concerns his father, who tries to "toughen him up" by playing the role of strict, unsympathetic disciplinarian, thereby only reinforcing the child's perceptions of inadequacy.

Mom will argue that her excessive attentiveness is needed to make up for her husband's strictness. Dad will argue that *someone* needs to draw the line for the boy, and it certainly isn't Mom! The message is clear even to the boy's classmates, who have taken to picking on him for his constant whining. But it is not clear to Mom.

Who Dresses Young Children?

Jane Nelsen, author of the POSITIVE DISCIPLINE series (Prima) and numerous other works, tells an interesting story drawn from her years as a school counselor working with little children and their parents. When a young child, five or six years old, was sent to her for counseling for some disciplinary matter, Dr. Nelsen asked the child: Who dresses you in the morning?

If the answer was Mom or Dad, Nelsen would immediately call the parents for a conference and attempt to renegotiate that arrangement. Her hope was that Mom and Dad would accept the challenge of working with the child and allowing him or her to learn how to get dressed. Yes, even five-year-olds can dress themselves when parents take time to help them organize their worlds, provide clothes that are easy to put on, and reflect parental confidence in their abilities.

A healthy self-concept develops out of experience and feedback, so the accomplishment of dressing oneself can be a powerful indicator of capability for a five-year-old. The challenge for parents is to avoid doing for very young children what they can do for themselves. Then, when they enter school, they will be accustomed to working

> ## School-Smart ParentingTip:
>
> ### Avoid doing for children what
> ### they can do for themselves!

through their own challenges and will be less likely to become frustrated with the unique challenges school will present.

Consider the story of Robert, who entered kindergarten and immediately impressed his teacher with his perfectly groomed and manicured appearance. His hair, in particular, was noticeable—picture-book blond, perfectly coifed, not a strand out of place. In appearance, he was the model student.

But before long Robert demonstrated unexpected negative qualities to his teacher. His attitude toward other students was surly and demeaning. He refused to do any work that he feared he could not do perfectly and better than anyone else. Temper tantrums were frequent.

And although these behaviors continued throughout Robert's kindergarten year (and in fact well into his later schooling), his teachers failed or refused to recognize that he was hurting inside. How could a child who looks so well groomed and whose parents obviously care so much about him be having behavioral problems? Maybe it's bad influence from the other children. Maybe he has an undiagnosed condition—allergies, migraines, Attention Deficit Disorder. Maybe he's just not being challenged . . . or maybe he is being challenged too much.

People failed to see that Robert's problems were in part due to the messages of inadequacy he was receiving from his parents. He couldn't comb his hair the way they thought it should be combed, so they combed it for him. He couldn't dress himself the way they thought he should be dressed, so they dressed him. He couldn't be relied upon to scrub his face and hands and neck to their satisfaction, so they did it for him.

In each of the above cases—the kindergartner in Jane Nelsen's story, the boy whose mom walks him to his chair each morning, and Robert with his perfectly combed hair—the parents are unaware of the real messages of inadequacy and worthlessness they are sending.

How important is it to encourage a sense of worth and adequacy? We believe it is absolutely essential! A healthy self-concept is the foundation of confidence, personal effectiveness, and self-esteem. Yes, it is *that* important!

"Power" is defined as the ability to act on one's own behalf. To "empower" is to create conditions that enable people to act—effectively—on their own behalf. Empowering children by helping them to see themselves as capable, worthy people will encourage them to find the confidence to face challenges and learn through experience. People who perceive themselves as capable believe that performing daily tasks and working through problems enables them to accumulate skills and gain wisdom. The belief that we are capable allows us to take the healthy risks involved in learning about ourselves and about life.

School-Smart Parenting Tip:

Celebrate effort rather than picking at results!

7

A Foundation of Initiative and Achievement

The word **"proactive"** is often used to describe the attitude that encourages us to take initiative and act on our own behalf. This proactive attitude is essential for developing a desire to initiate and achieve. Our self-concept develops as a result of our experiences, combined with our own internal processing of those experiences and helpful and supportive feedback from others. Perceiving oneself as capable is fundamental to developing a healthy self-concept, which leads to developing attitudes and skills for effective living and learning.

When significant adults show respect for a child's ability to learn and face challenges, the child is more likely to develop the perception that he or she has the ability to succeed. Unfortunately, many traditional ways of dealing with children reflect lack of respect for and confidence in their capability, which in turn gives rise to unnecessary barriers to their development.

▼

Chapter

2

Barriers and Builders

Children often find, in the eyes of parents and teachers, mirrors in which they discover themselves!

—Ancient Wisdom

We have identified a number of behaviors adults commonly use when dealing with children that undercut the development of a healthy self-concept and therefore *reduce* children's confidence and ability to learn. For this reason, we call these behaviors "barriers." We have also identified alternative behaviors that build a healthy self-concept and therefore *increase* children's confidence and ability to learn. We call these "builders."

As we begin our journey toward understanding how to more effectively raise children for success and happiness in school, let's look at how barriers and builders can affect the lives of young people in school-related situations.

9

▼ Barrier #1 . . . Negative or Limiting Assumptions

When we are too quick to assume what children will think or do, how they will feel or act, how they will respond to challenges and situations, or what they can or cannot accomplish for themselves, and deal with them accordingly we create barriers to the development of their sense of competency. For example: "I didn't tell you about it because you *always* get upset!" You *never* think that I _____!" or "You are too little to _____!"

The mom who unpacks her son's book bag every day is assuming that the boy cannot succeed at that task without her. She assumes that because he needed her to walk him to class on the first day of school, he has learned nothing since then and will continue to need her to walk him to class every day. She assumes that love requires her to constantly do things for her son—even things he could very well do for himself.

Imagine what Helen Keller's life might have been like as a deaf and blind person had not Anne Sullivan come along and persuaded Helen's parents to stop assuming they had to take care of everything for her. When they learned to back off and let her fend for herself, she demonstrated incredible ability—even learning to speak and write in a language she had never heard, about a world that she had never seen.

Limited thinking on the part of the parent can result in limited thinking on the part of the child. For example: "I knew you would not be interested in that so I didn't tell you about it," "I didn't tell you about it because you always get upset," or "I took care of it myself because . . . I can't count on you to take responsibility for it!"

Assuming is, unfortunately, a natural reaction. It is typical to assume what our children need in terms of what they needed yesterday . . . or a year ago. It is normal to assume that our children will be interested in the same things we are interested in, and nothing else. It is natural to assume that we know what's best for them. But, however natural this assumption, it is also limiting. It stunts growth, which comes for us and for our children when we take the time to question our assumptions. Questioning rather than assuming may well begin all learning.

▼ Builder #1 . . . Checking

When we begin with the assumption that people grow and change from day to day and may have capabilities and resources of which we are unaware, we approach each situation as a unique opportunity. We try to actively and optimistically mirror a belief in people's potential. We encourage people to see life as a process of becoming. We might say, for example: "What, if any, help would you like?" "How would you like to deal with this situation now?" "Let me check out where you are on this issue now," or "Give it a try and let's see how it goes this time!"

The first-grader who stopped his dad at the school door and told him he could find his own way to his classroom is the exception. With most children, we need to check things out. Instead of walking the boy into the classroom, the over-indulgent mom could have asked her little son what he needs: "Son, usually I walk you into your classroom and unpack your book bag for you. But I've noticed how big you've grown lately, and I thought I might ask you what you'd like me to do today?"

If he answers "I don't know," she could help him with "Would it be okay if I just walked you into the school building today and let you handle it from there? I know you can do it." How much more encouraging that parent would be than the one who continually assumes no growth has taken place!

When we avoid binding people to their history, they often surprise us with their capacity to grow. Instead of "You always think . . . !" or "I can never count on you to . . . !" how about "How would you like to handle this today?" or "What are your thoughts about . . . ?"

▼ *Barrier #2 . . . Rescuing/Explaining*

Stepping in to take care of problems or issues before a child has had a chance to experience them or to try and work them out him- or herself, conveys these messages: You do not believe the child can handle problems and you are more interested in seeing situations resolved than in the child's opportunity to learn from them. Setting aside results or consequences, rather than helping children face and learn to deal with them, reduces their confidence and accountability.

Providing explanations for children so that they do not learn to think things through and develop explanations of their own, teaches them to be intellectually dependent and reduces their confidence as learners.

Rescuing may be the most prevalent barrier in our society. The mom who runs to school to deliver her child's forgotten homework, the dad who time and again intercedes with the teachers to bail his daughter out of some disciplinary situation she got herself into, the teacher who fails to follow through on a reasonable consequence for behavior—all are saying: "You are not capable of experiencing and learning from the consequences of your choices; therefore, I must step in and rescue you."

Rescuing is the barrier that adults often set up to prevent young people from experiencing the trauma of thinking and making decisions on their own. The dad who reviews his son's report card and insists on explaining what the boy did poorly, is rescuing the child from an opportunity to learn self-assessment and problem-solving skills that are major confidence builders. In chapter 16, "The No-Rescue Contract," we will look at a creative way that many schools around the country are formalizing the process of discouraging rescuing.

▼ Builder #2 . . . Exploring

When we avoid stepping in to take care of matters that children need to learn to deal with, we encourage them to discover and develop their capabilities. We allow them to take acceptable risks and face new challenges in order to have experiences from which they can learn.

Instead of doing their thinking for them and explaining what happened, what caused it to happen, and what they should do differently, explore these issues with children by asking questions that enable them to develop their own understanding. Instead of emphasizing what happened, emphasize what was learned from the experience. Instead of rescuing, stand back and allow the child to work through the problem herself, knowing that no time will be as safe as now for her to make a mistake and learn from it. And if she stumbles, be patient and use the experience as a teachable moment.

When she calls home because she forgot her homework, resist the impulse to run to school; instead, stand firm while expressing empathy and understanding: "Honey, I'm sorry you forgot to take your homework to school, and I appreciate your concern, but you'll need to work through this as best you can. When you get home, if you'd like we can explore together a more effective plan for remembering to bring all your materials to school."

The builder, exploring, allows us to work with children, helping them achieve greater understanding of their experiences. By asking children questions in a supportive, nonjudgmental setting when they have problems, we build their confidence as learners:

Parent: What happened yesterday?

Child: I never got around to organizing my things last night.

Parent: What caused you to neglect to organize your things last night?

Child: I just got involved on the phone talking to Annie for too long, and before I knew it was time for bed.

Parent: How can you use what you learned from this to get yourself organized for tomorrow?

Child: Decide on a time limit for talking to Annie.

It has been said that "Teaching consists of causing or allowing people to get into situations from which they cannot escape except through thinking." To that, we would add: "and then bringing forth the learner's understanding!" (Remember that the Latin root of the word educate is *educe,* which means "to bring forth.")

School-Smart Parenting Tip:

When we learn to be "midwives" in the birth of children's understanding, we empower them as capable learners!

▼ *Barrier #3 . . . Directing*

Directing can mean taking too much responsibility for deciding what needs to be done, then telling others what to do, or issuing arbitrary orders when the consequences don't justify it; or having an overly controlling attitude and treating people as objects to be moved about at your pleasure; or demanding compliance rather than inviting assistance.

Do you know parents who part company with their children each morning, sending them away from their family for eight hours, away from those who love and care for them more than anyone else in the world, with words such as these: "Now don't forget to button your coat, and be nice to your sister on the school bus, and remember to eat the vegetables I packed for you, and don't forget you've got your chores to do when you get home . . ."? Is it any wonder our children tune us out?

Do you know parents who insist on determining where, when, and under what conditions their children will do their homework, rather than working with the children to determine *their* preferred place, *their* preferred time, and *their* preferred learning environment? Or do you know parents who sit side by side with their children, directing them how to complete every part of their homework?

Do you know parents who insist on answering *for* their children, telling them what to say, when to say it, and how to say it? Does the following dialogue sound familiar?

Neighbor: Hi, honey, what's your name?
Mom: Say "Stacie."
Stacie: (mumbling) Stacie.
Neighbor: And how old are you, Stacie?
Mom: Say "Four."
Stacie: (barely audible) Four.
Neighbor: And is that a new dress you're wearing?
Mom: Say "Yes, Mommy picked it out for me yesterday."
Stacie: (completely inaudible now) Yes, Mommy picked it out for me yesterday.
Mom: Speak up, dear, and answer the nice lady's questions.
Stacie: (to herself) Why should I? You always answer for me!

These parents place concern for the task ahead of empowerment for the child. Directing may fulfill the adults' need to be in control, to ensure that everything is done their way. And, it works . . . for short-term results. But in the long run, it produces dependency, reduces initiative, generates passive-aggressive behavior, reduces cooperation, increases resentment, and encourages disrespect—none of which contribute to a child's sense of competency.

▼ Builder #3 . . . Inviting/Encouraging

When we see children as capable, we show respect for their need to learn how to plan and organize tasks and participate in problem solving. We encourage them to think things through and invite their contributions and/or assistance in getting things done. We show tolerance and appreciation for ideas other than our own because we know that their contributions will foster commitment and cooperation. Instead of telling people what to do, we explore their ideas and plans for getting something done. Instead of viewing children as objects we control, we view them as resourceful people we value.

Like all the barriers, directing is an easy habit to get into and a difficult one to break. In our struggle to change the behavior pattern of directing, it is helpful to remember that significant improvement is possible when we just do nothing. When we simply stop, even in mid-sentence, and refrain from verbally taking control of children, we allow positive change to occur.

If, for example, through my son's entire elementary school experience, I reminded him after dinner to do his homework, then upon his entry to middle school I decide not to, he will probably say to me, "Dad, you forgot to remind me to do my homework." Then I can say, "Son, it's taken me much longer than it should have, but I've finally realized that you're a pretty capable guy. I know that you can take care of getting your homework done, so I've decided it's not respectful for me to assume you can't do it without my direction." This communicates my recognition of the growth that has taken place in him and conveys my confidence that he can remember on his own.

But I can go even further than this by practicing the builder of encouraging. This proactive approach communicates confidence and provides opportunities for the child to perceive himself as an asset rather than just the target of my directions or recipient of my rescuing.

I can say to my son (the beginning of a new school year is a perfect opportunity for this): "Thomas, last year I reminded you every day after dinner that it was time for you to do your homework. This year I'd like to chat with you about your homework and ask you when you most prefer to do it, where you'd like to do it, how you'd like to remind yourself to do it, and about any other details you think are important."

How much more encouraging that would be! No, it may not come easily. And, yes, it does take practice. But the payoff is a more capable, self-confident young person who can initiate problem solving on his own and learn to organize what needs to be done.

▼ Barrier #4 . . . Expecting "Too Much, Too Soon!"

This means using the potential you see in children as a standard by which to judge them and their performance in the present, and then faulting them for falling short of your expectations.

It may involve "shoulding" children for their less-than-perfect performance; demanding "too much, too soon" so they become discouraged and refuse to try for fear they will fail, do things unsatisfactorily, or look bad; emphasizing the outcome rather than what was gained from the attempt. Expecting too much may be expressed in the following ways: "Do it right . . . or don't do it at all!" "You *should* know that already!" "I *expected* more of you . . . than this!" "Surely you can see that this is not the *right* way to go about something!"

The barrier of expecting too much, too soon is particularly prevalent in school-related situations, largely due to the high expectations most American parents hold for their children. It appears when we use the potential we see in children as a standard by which to judge them, then criticize their failure to "live up to" their potential at this moment.

Michael (as a principal) once observed a teacher conduct a forty-five-minute math class with thirty-five eighth-graders during which not a sound was made by the students; not even a whisper broke the pervading silence of the room. Never had he observed a group of fourteen-year-olds so on task, so attuned to their responsibilities. He was genuinely impressed.

At the close of the class, he asked the teacher what her secret for classroom management and discipline was; he will never forget her response: "Not one of these students will ever receive from me the highest allowable grade for conduct. That is reserved for sainthood. None of them will ever reach the standard I set for them. But they're too scared to strive for anything less!"

This teacher had set her expectations so impossibly high that no one could meet them. It reminds one of Mark Twain's commentary about the preacher who, in a blistering hellfire-and-damnation sermon, succeeded in reducing the number of the elect to a figure so small it was hardly worth the saving.

This teacher had reduced the number of students who, in her eyes, were behaving at an exemplary level to zero. To follow her logic here is interesting: I expect nothing but the most perfect discipline in my classroom; but being flawed individuals, none of us is capable of perfection on this earth. Therefore, no student of mine will ever be recognized as worthy of the highest allowable conduct grade. This frightening example illustrates the barrier of expecting too much taken to absurd lengths.

Ah, but it worked! The kids were so well behaved! So on task! So absorbed in their work! Yes, to the superficial observer (such as Michael at the time), it did work. But a trained observer would have noticed that beneath the surface, the students had one goal on their minds: How can I get through this class without being called on or forced to participate? How can I last forty-five minutes without being seen? How can I make myself inconspicuous? How can I survive with my self-esteem intact?

There are two roads for a young person to take when confronted by such a teacher: rebellion or retreat. These students were too terrified, or conditioned, to rebel; the only road that remained was retreat.

But did they learn math? Well, they learned enough to keep the teacher away from them! But only that much. They learned not to question, not to try different paths, not to collaborate with others, and not to make intelligent guesses, lest they draw attention to themselves. To question, to try different paths, to collaborate with others, and to make intelligent guesses—the essence of math processing—were all lost on this classroom of students.

But they were so well behaved! Again, on the surface it appeared so. What this teacher didn't know, or didn't care about, was how these students behaved when she was not around. They were, in fact, the terrors of the school. No other teacher could handle them. Unable to fulfill her expectations of perfection, they took the opposite route and fulfilled the one expectation they *could* fulfill—being terrors. Once outside her room, they wrought havoc on everyone else. Who could blame them?

We all—teachers particularly—need to hold high expectations for what children can accomplish, irrespective of what the student's past experience has demonstrated.

But it is critical that we understand this process as based on hope, optimism, and encouragement! We want third-graders to fulfill all the social, emotional, physical, and intellectual growth expected of third-graders . . . as soon as each is able to do so—not by 9 A.M. on the first day of the school year!

Indeed, study after study indicates that children do rise in a climate of positive, encouraging expectations and fall in a climate of discounts and judgmentalism. When we convey the message to young people that they are inadequate because they do not meet our expectations, they are tempted to live out that inadequacy.

▼ Builder #4 . . . Celebrating

When we see children's potential as possibilities waiting to be discovered rather than requirements for what they should or shouldn't be now, we create a safe climate for risking growth and learning. We are alert for signs of progress and respond to them with genuine enthusiasm. Effort and improvement are treated as more valuable than success or failure, and we emphasize "more effective" and "less effective" ways to act rather than stress the absolutes of "right way" and "wrong way" whenever possible.

When Thomas Edison finally came up with the electric light bulb, someone said, "How do you look back on your thousands of failures now that you have finally succeeded?" He responded, "None of them could have been failures or I wouldn't have succeeded . . . each project was an opportunity to learn something that made this moment possible." The only failure would have been failure to *try* or failure to *learn* from each experiment!

When we reflect optimistic perceptions of children's ability to learn and grow, they generally move toward their potential. As Henry Ford said, "If you believe you can, or if you believe you can't . . . you're right!" Children become more willing to participate in discussions and face challenges when they believe their effort and improvement will be appreciated and celebrated. They learn to see achievement as not just accomplishment, but as a process of taking small steps, each of which adds to their capabilities.

In 1987, the United States Department of Labor awarded a $1.3 million grant to the American Society for Training and Development to research training needs and assess current training activities in corporations across the United States. One result of that study was the identification of four key skills common to successful learners in universities and in the business world. One of these—the ability to break down complex tasks into manageable parts—adds a teaching dimension to the importance of celebrating what one gains from trying. (The other three skills were asking questions, looking for feedback, and focusing on goals.)

School-Smart Parenting Tip:

**Encourage your children to divide
new tasks they are learning into
smaller, more manageable parts.**

When we take the time to celebrate what children gain from an experience, we not only contribute to their sense of competency, we also encourage them to develop a key to successful learning: *breaking down large tasks into smaller, more manageable components.*

▼ *Barrier #5 . . . Adultisms*

It has been said that "'isms' are viruses that destroy human society." In medicine, chronic degenerative conditions are often called "isms" (alcoholism and astigmatism, for example). In human relationships, "diseases" of intolerance are often called "isms" (racism, sexism, judgmentalism, hedonism, pessimism). When we judge children (based on a stereotype) as being less worthy of respect because they are different from us, we commit an "adultism."

When an adult (who was once a child) forgets what it was like to be a child and then criticizes or discounts a child (who has never been an adult) for not thinking, seeing, acting, doing, feeling, or responding as an adult, we call it an "adultism." An adult who commits adultism might say, for example: "You're too young to appreciate . . . ." "Children should be seen and not heard!" "No child of mine will ever . . . ." "When will you ever grow up?" "Why are you so childish?!"

Adultism is the language we use when we communicate to children that they are at fault for not seeing what we see, for not understanding at the same level we do. Once, when Michael was about sixteen years old (and knew everything there was to know), he somehow got stuck tutoring a younger sister in math. Because she was younger, and a girl, she was, by his definition, ignorant. When she failed to understand a particular math problem as quickly as he thought she should, he exploded: "It's obvious! You're just too young to understand it!"

An uncle who was visiting at the time—a patient, kind gentleman—commented: "Michael, it's obvious to you. It's not obvious to Rita. Why don't you ask her to share with you what she *does* understand about the problem. Then maybe you can guide her from there." Michael doesn't remember taking this advice—after all, why would he need advice when he knew everything?—but his uncle's suggestion stayed with him.

Adultisms are basically "put downs," statements that reflect to children that they occupy a lower level of the universe than we do, and therefore are not worthy of the respect we want for ourselves. Adultisms are easily recognizable—just ask yourself whether you would speak the same way to a friend. If not, it's probably an adultism.

▼ Builder #5 . . . Respecting

When we avoid stereotypes about such issues as gender, race, and age, and see each person as a unique individual worthy of the same respect and consideration we expect for ourselves, we encourage collaboration and understanding. We show tolerance for, and interest in, diverse ways of thinking, feeling, and acting. Instead of arguing over whose perception is "right," or discounting people for not seeing things the way they "should," we acknowledge that it is possible that *both* perceptions are valid and then explore mutually respectful possibilities.

> **School-Smart Parenting Tip:**
> Children who are not judged, discounted, or humiliated for their perceptions (or for being children) are more likely to trust the communication process and respond to adults as mentors and role models.

Adultisms include those tired, worn-out putdowns and demeaning expressions our own parents sometimes hurled at us when we were young—those we swore never to use against our own children. But we do. We continue to use them because we have not consciously identified possible substitutes.

Counselors say that people overcoming addiction have a greater chance of success when they substitute healthy alternatives for addiction. To "just say no" is not enough; we need a specific alternative to the addictive activity to succeed. So too with adultisms.

The alternative to adultism is respect. Just as adultism could be defined as the language one uses when engaging in the previous four barriers, respectfulness could be defined as the language we demonstrate when using the builders. A helpful rule of thumb in evaluating the expressions we use is this: Would I want a friend to speak to me like this? If not, what expression would be more respectful?

For example, when my child complains to me about perceived mistreatment, I might be tempted to respond: "That's too bad. No one ever said life is fair." But would I respond that way to an adult friend? More likely, I would respond with empathy rather than disregard. For example: "I'm sorry to hear that. I can tell it is very upsetting to you." Which response is more respectful? Children are people who deserve our respect as much as our friends do.

One of the most common age stereotypes is "teenager." When we say "Teenagers . . . (this)" or "Teenagers . . . (that)," we are saying: "The most important characteristic of this person is the '1' that begins their age." Yet, if we think about it, we all know mature, responsible 13-year-olds (children) and immature and irresponsible 19-year-olds (men or women). We all know 16-year-old moderates, 15-year-old conservatives, and 17-year-old liberals. The actual *people* behind these numbers do not fit any stereotype. A strong developmental need of adolescents is to "individuate"—break out of the mold of childhood and achieve the status of an individual in their own right. Therefore, it is healthier for everyone when adults think of adolescents as "young people" and give them credit and respect for their individuality!

Do we create barriers through such stereotyping? The bad news is that we do, and they spring up so easily. With no effort on our part, and often with no ill intention, we manage to erect these barriers that hold back the development of young people. But the good news is that much can be accomplished by simply creating such barriers less often or, better yet, by avoiding them altogether. By simply *not* assuming that a child is inadequate, by *not* rescuing him when he forgets his lunch, by *not* directing her every action, by *not* expecting children to achieve their full potential right now, and by refraining from disrespectful adultisms, we can make giant strides toward instilling within our children a sense of their capability.

Avoid the Barriers	Use the Builders
Assuming	Checking
Rescuing/Explaining	Exploring
Directing	Encouraging/Inviting
Expecting Too Much, Too Soon	Celebrating
Using Adultisms	Respecting

Children's perceptions of their capabilities are enhanced when significant people in their lives take time to work *with* them by checking, exploring, encouraging, celebrating, and respecting, rather than working *for* or *against* them by assuming, rescuing, directing, expecting, and using adultisms. The first step in learning how to prepare children for success and happiness in school is to avoid erecting barriers to their perceiving themselves as capable, and to practice using appropriate builders.

School-Smart Parenting Tip:
Learn to replace "barrier behaviors"
with "builder behaviors"!

Our next step is to move beyond the attitude we project and look carefully at the specific perceptions and skills our children need in order to develop into capable, effective students who can act on their own behalf with responsibility and integrity. Our study of exceptionally capable, effective people led to our identifying seven essential characteristics, which form the basis of *7 Strategies for Developing Capable Students*. Let's take a look at each of the seven, and learn to implement all of them as we help our children develop as capable students.

▼

Chapter

3

The Significant Seven

I think I'm making progress!
—Pablo Casals (responding to a reporter's question about why, at age ninety-five, he still practices the cello six hours a day)

During Michael's college years, he spent summers cleaning recently vacated apartments, getting them ready for new residents. Two of his colleagues on the job reflected opposite views of life: pessimism and optimism.

Pessimism

One of the "lifers" on the job was an older fellow who complained incessantly. The boss was always mistreating him, the government was conspiring against him, and his wife would never cook his favorite meals. His kids were no good, the weather was insufferable, and the new uniforms they made us wear looked ridiculous. He complained interminably about the job, and always gave reasons why another person's suggestions for making things better wouldn't work. Life was one long series of events that made him miserable and were out of his control.

One day Michael risked asking the pessimist whether he had ever thought about looking for another job, since he obviously hated this one. "No," he said. "I tried once. Decided to become a firefighter. But when I sat down to take the test, I read the first question—'What is atmospheric pressure at sea level?'—and I said to myself, 'How would *I* know what atmospheric pressure is at sea level? Who *cares* what atmospheric pressure is at sea level? What does that have to do with fighting fires?' So I walked out right then . . . and I've been working here ever since."

Well, while the importance of a firefighter knowing about atmospheric pressure at sea level is not clear, one can't help thinking that the person who quits a test after the first question would probably drive up to a raging fire and say, "Forget it! That fire's out of control. It's no use even *trying* to stop it. I'm going home."

Persistence

On the same job, Michael had a friend who was determined to become a police officer. This fellow was using the money he earned cleaning apartments to finish college so he could enhance his chances of being accepted at the police academy. This friend was no scholar, but his mind was set on completing his college education, then applying for the police force. During breaks, all he talked about was getting college behind him and becoming a cop.

Well, he did get the college behind him—just barely. Four times he had to repeat classes he had failed. He retook the classes at night, on weekends, and even once on weekdays during the summer, negotiating with the apartment boss so he could come to work later on class days. Once he even hired a tutor, using his own money, to help him through a particularly difficult statistics class. Upon graduation, he applied immediately to the police academy. He sailed through the physical and psychological testing, and his character review was flawless; but because he failed to meet the minimum standard in the academic testing, the academy turned him down.

Undaunted, he went to the library, checked out books on how to pass civil service exams, and embarked on an intensive self-study program. He carried the books with him wherever he went, studied every opportunity he got, passed up numerous opportunities for "happy hour," reapplied to the police academy exam, took the test, and, this time, passed. He was accepted, went through training, qualified, and is now a detective with a big city police force.

What Makes the Difference?

Why do some people tend to use experiences as opportunities to learn while others use similar experiences as excuses to quit? What factors in one person's make-up encourage him or her to bounce back from negative experiences while another person uses negative experiences to justify his state in life? What prepares some to see life in terms of challenges and opportunities that are subject to their influence, while others see life in terms of problems that are caused by other people and are largely beyond their capacity to influence?

In pursuit of answers to questions like these, we have spent years studying exceptionally capable, resilient people. Our studies have increasingly focused on three perceptions and four skills (The Significant Seven) that are essential to dealing with all of life's facets.

Weakness in these seven life resources correlates with problems such as decline in motivation and achievement in school, dropping out of school, drug and alcohol abuse, promiscuity, and gang involvement. Increasing strength in the seven areas directly correlates with health, productivity, personal effectiveness, and achievement. Like physically strong people (who tend to bounce back from illness), those who exhibit sufficient strength in the identified perceptions and skills tend to thrive on challenges and adversity. Those who are weak or inadequate in these areas are typically overwhelmed by adversity and defeated by challenge.

Resiliency, or the ability to "thrive under adverse or challenging circumstances," is as critical to effectiveness in school as it is to other aspects of life. For example, a child who receives an "F" on a test, then proceeds to assess the situation by asking herself "What happened?" "What may have contributed to the outcome?" and "What did I learn from this that will help me do better next time?" shows courage, optimism, and willingness to learn—all qualities of resilience. The odds are that she will do better on her next test. On the other hand, a child who gets the "F," then blames it on the teacher, her parents (for not helping her), or any number of external factors is yielding initiative to circumstance. As a result, she becomes increasingly at risk of failing subsequent tests.

Following is a list of **The Significant Seven,** each accompanied by a statement that one who possesses the attribute might make.

SEVEN RESOURCES OF
EXCEPTIONALLY CAPABLE STUDENTS

1. Strong Perceptions of Personal Capabilities
"I am a capable person who can face problems and challenges and gain strength and wisdom through experience."

2. Strong Perceptions of Personal Significance

"Who I am and what I have to offer in life and relationships is of value—my life has meaning and purpose."

3. Strong Perceptions of Personal Influence

"I am accountable for my actions and choices, and I have the power to influence my life!"

4. Strong Intrapersonal Skills

"I am acquiring the skills of self-assessment, self-control, and self-discipline in responding to and dealing with feelings."

5. Strong Interpersonal Skills

"I am acquiring the skills to communicate, cooperate, negotiate, share, empathize, resolve conflicts, and listen effectively when dealing with people!"

6. Strong Systemic Skills

"I am acquiring the skills to be sufficiently responsible, adaptable, and flexible—able to function effectively within systems (including societal, legal, familial, educational, environmental)."

7. Strong Judgment Skills

"I am developing the skills and resources for planning, identifying choices, and making decisions based on experience and moral and ethical principles—such as honesty, respect, fairness, equality, and compassion—all essential to developing 'mature judgment.' "

The process of building strength in The Significant Seven perceptions and skills provides the foundation for *7 Strategies for Developing Capable Students*. As we review these perceptions and skills in the following pages, ask yourself what behaviors you wish to practice and what changes you want to make to further promote them in your home.

▼

Chapter

4

Developing Strong Perceptions of Personal Capabilities

Sir Winston . . . what, in your school experience, best prepared you to lead Great Britain out of her darkest hour?
(thoughtful pause)
It was the two years I spent in the First Form (seventh grade).
Did you fail the First Form?
No! I had two opportunities to learn to do it correctly!

—Sir Winston Churchill

The "builders" described in chapter 1 provide tremendous support for developing one's perception of personal capability. When we encourage children to take initiative, face challenges, and learn from experience, we show belief in their capabilities and ensure them opportunities to discover and validate their resourcefulness.

Have you ever noticed how eager young children are to try new things? To show that they can do things for themselves? "Me can do it!" they may say.

Sometimes we unwittingly suppress their eagerness with phrases such as "You're too little!" or "Wait until you can do it right!" rather than encourage their efforts and celebrate whatever they do. Many of children's perceptions of themselves are based on what they think adults think of them.

Perceptions are unique to each human being and develop cumulatively through analyzing experiences and attaching personal meaning to them. When we explain experiences for others instead of encouraging them to explore their own perceptions first, we miss opportunities to help them enhance their sense of being capable.

People learn to see themselves as capable when those who raise, teach, or work with them think they are capable and treat them that way. **Children often see themselves as they think others see them.** Parents and teachers can promote children's positive self-perception by focusing on capabilities.

Children who hear phrases such as "Why can't you ever? How come you never? Surely you realize! How many times do I have to tell you? When will you grow up?" may interpret this as evidence of their lack of capability. Such negative comments imply that actions are synonymous with people. This encourages individuals to feel that they are incompetent, incapable, and unsuccessful because they don't do things consistently well.

Adults who view themselves as capable find it easier to treat children or students as capable. Because children or students tend to learn from what they see, they are more likely to adopt a positive self-perception from adults who identify themselves as capable. A supremely competent parent/teacher, however, may intimidate and discourage a child through unreasonably high expectations. Children who believe they are capable work at gaining wisdom through experience. They recognize that they can often learn as much from mistakes as from successes. They see themselves as able to work through problems and situations, even against difficult odds.

To encourage this kind of thinking in children, we can learn to structure situations so that children can gain essential experience and learn to recognize healthy role models and behaviors. We can then encourage them to become their own role models by exploring questions such as "What is it that you admire about the way that person behaves?" "Why is that worth respecting or admiring?" and "How can you learn to incorporate these ideas and behaviors into your life?"

The little boy that Michael overheard expressing confidence that he didn't need his dad's help is a wonderful example of a developing capable young person. We did not watch him enter the classroom, but can imagine him walking directly to his seat, getting out the books, and saying to himself, "Okay, Mrs. Grady, I'm here to learn whatever you've got to teach; give me the chance."

We don't know the boy's parents, but would guess they've raised him to see himself as a capable person. We would bet they involve him in family chores and affirm his contributions as significant to the family. They probably actively validate him in his uniqueness, listen to him when he talks about his own interests, encourage him to explore his world, ask him questions that call for meaningful responses, give him choices in his daily activities, support him when he makes mistakes, and answer questions he asks.

It's easy to imagine an emotionally stable home, with rituals and traditions that celebrate effort, support a sense of family, and encourage mutual respect. These parents probably make as many mistakes as the rest of us, but strive to learn from those mistakes and model, to the best of their abilities, the behaviors most important to them.

If you were to predict that young boy's future, it's easy to foresee a student with a level of confidence that would allow him to accept each challenge presented to him as one more opportunity to demonstrate his abilities. When he gets stuck, he will probably focus his efforts, test other methods, and call upon the support of others.

You can imagine him thriving not only with effective teachers, but with not-so-effective teachers as well, because he has learned that what he accomplishes in life is largely dependent upon his own efforts. You can see a young boy who sees himself as a capable student.

So how can we help children perceive themselves as capable students? Avoid communicating to them that their acceptability and worthiness of love is conditional or in any way affected by their performance, and that their worth and identity is in any way influenced by their grades.

Avoid describing them in terms of their grades. A common mistake is for a teacher or parent to refer to a child as a "B-student" or a "C-student," as if the letter grade somehow defines them. Some students more frequently than not get "A's," and others more frequently than not get "D's"; but that does not make the former an "A-student" or the latter a "D-student." **Speak of their school work as their work . . . not their identity.** "He/she is doing 'A' work . . . under this teacher . . . in this subject . . . this year!"

School-Smart Parenting Tip:
Teach children to associate learning with life and experience, not only with school!

Teach children that they can learn anywhere in life, especially when they set a learning goal for themselves and take the initiative to gain the necessary knowledge and skills to accomplish that goal. We can demonstrate our confidence, with empathy, to encourage children to succeed with difficult tasks.

The parent who responds to a child's difficulty with homework by saying, "You're in the sixth grade and you can't add fractions! Why, when I was in school we learned addition of fractions in the fourth grade!" is not helping. But neither is the parent who says, "Fractions in the sixth grade? That's terrible! That's much too hard for you! What's wrong with that school?"

The former response is demeaning, leading to poor self-concept and a lack of confidence. But the latter is likewise demeaning, because it suggests that the child is not capable of meeting school standards, which also leads to low levels of confidence and self-esteem. A more effective approach would be along these lines:

Bobby: I just can't get this addition of fractions stuff. Mrs. Nichols is too hard. Nobody understands this.

Mom: Adding fractions can be difficult. I can understand your frustration. I remember having some problems with it when I was in school, too. What do you think you can do to help yourself understand it?

Bobby: Nothin'. I might as well just forget it and flunk sixth grade.

Mom: Well, that's one option. But maybe there are others. What would happen if you went to see Mrs. Nichols after school for a little help? Or asked your friend Joey to help you?

Bobby: I've got a better idea. Why don't you just show me how to do it?

Mom: I'll tell you what. Why don't you show me what you *do* know, and then I'll try to guide you from there.

What is Mom accomplishing here? She is affirming and validating Bobby's feelings by communicating empathy, she is helping him think of choices, and she is building on his current knowledge to guide him further.

If she is wise, she will resist the temptation to become his teacher at this point. She will make an effort to understand what Bobby has already learned from the teacher and will guide him accordingly. She might have him go back to his favorite homework place and, after completing a few problems, check one or two; but she must be careful that Bobby does not depend on her to do the checking.

Often children just want to know that we care enough to empathize with their struggle and give them some time. Asking the child what he already knows and supporting that with patience is frequently all he needs to get going on his own.

We communicate to children that they are capable people when we express confidence that they can make progress through working at tasks. Homework and other projects are opportunities to actively cultivate children's abilities to persist and learn independently. As we work patiently with them as they struggle to learn the lessons of life—academic and otherwise—we raise more confident problem-solvers who can meet life's challenges.

> ## School-Smart Parenting Tip:
> **Validate effort, initiative, and persistence . . . rather than ability!**

Current research indicates that children who are told they are "good at" something tend to concentrate on that skill and often will not show interest in or try other activities. They often rationalize poor performance by saying they are just "not good at that." Children who are given recognition for trying new things and who receive specific recognition for effort and persistence typically achieve more and develop a wider range of interests and abilities.

▼

Chapter

5

Developing Strong Perceptions of Personal Significance

*Most addictive, compulsive behaviors and the vast majority of so-
called "unwanted" pregnancies may actually represent an attempt, on
the individual's part, to fill a void of significance within the core of
their identity!*

—Rollo May

A mom, in the depths of frustration, was heard to ex-
claim about her son: "Timmy is a negative cash flow!"
Timmy had recently broken a window in the house, and
last week had lost a brand-new overcoat that had cost the
family a modest investment. Timmy was indeed a negative cash flow.

Back in the 1930s, when two out of three American
families lived in rural areas, not many children would be

viewed as "negative cash flows." Most children were needed in the family economy, and chores were real-life activities representing real family needs—gathering the eggs, milking the cows, planting and harvesting the crops, and so on. In such families, children were very much "positive cash flows" and significant contributors.

But today, unless parents actively engage children in meaningful activities that contribute to the well-being of the family, that is not the case. Viewed strictly from a financial perspective, our children typically add little if anything to the household economy, serving only as debits on the family balance sheet.

Of course, it would be reprehensible for parents to see their children solely in terms of their financial benefit to the family. That is not our point here. Our point relates to how children see themselves in relation to the family, not how we see them. Do they see themselves as contributors? Do they see themselves as important members of the family team, with specific things to offer? Do they see themselves as necessary to the wholeness of the family, such that if they were absent the family would be less? Or . . . do they see themselves as negative cash flows?

The strongest human need may well be to perceive this: "I am a significant person whose life has meaning and purpose; I contribute in meaningful ways; and I am needed." Plenty of evidence supports the fact that virtually every aspect of physical, mental, and social health is influenced by whether this need is or is not fulfilled.

School-Smart Parenting Tip:
Ask not what you can do for
your children . . . but what meaningful
things your children can do for
themselves, you, and others!

Gerontologists often recommend pets and house plants for their patients who no longer have family members around. One reason is that people who believe that something "needs" them to care for it will generally have better health, less depression, and a longer life expectancy. For the same reason, children who contribute to the care of pets, older relatives, or younger siblings are less likely to drop out of school, get involved with drug abuse, or join gangs.

Human beings appear among the few creatures for whom the need to perceive significance in one's life is stronger than the drive for physical survival. Human beings may commit suicide—or lose the will to live, the resistance to disease and depression, or the motivation to progress—when they believe they or their lives are insignificant.

Three Conditions

Three conditions appear necessary for any relationship or experience to meet the human need for significance:

1. To be listened to (understanding)
2. To be taken seriously with respect to feelings, thoughts, and ideas (acceptance)
3. To be genuinely needed as a contributor (affirmation)

Appropriate attitudes and dialogue are crucial in meeting the first two conditions. When our attitudes are that children's thoughts and ideas are important, then we commit time to the process of communication. When we show interest in what is important to them; when we learn to talk *with* them—rather than *at* them, *to* them, or *for* them (as so many adults do)—then we both affirm them as significant and strengthen their skills in dialogue and communication through modeling.

When we avoid sarcasm, criticism, and other discounting dialogue, we show acceptance. When we avoid being judgmental about mistakes, errors, and immature behavior and use encouragement and problem-solving instead, we teach self-acceptance. When we make our love and care for each child unconditional and treat what they do simply as what they do (not who they are), we contribute greatly to their sense of significance.

Whenever children make contributions of time, effort, or consideration, we can respond with specific recognition and feedback. For example: "Your doing ____ was particularly helpful to me today because I was feeling _____." This way children will know your affirmation is sincere and what about their efforts made them contributions rather than just chores.

One differentiation between chores and contributions is that it is *how* the activity is perceived by the actor rather than *what* the activity is that determines its potential for affirmation. Chores are a necessary part of life. However, when children help (through participating in family meetings, for example) identify what needs to be done, determine the reasons these chores are important, and think of ways to get them done, they are more likely to view chores as contributions. When children choose what they are willing to be responsible for (rather than just having them assigned), they tend to see what they do as more significant.

Family/class meetings and other collaborative activities such as rituals and traditions can be excellent opportunities for young people to experience being active contributing members of a family or a class. These events also celebrate both the family and its individual members.

The perception that one is a significant, contributing member of groups and institutions of which he or she is a member has critical applications in school. For example, Fred was always getting into trouble for graffiti and other "unsolicited" artwork around the school (and the community). He had been suspended twice and was developing a negative, resistant attitude toward teachers and school in general, and showed little interest in school activities. On several occasions he was given after-school detention and, on one occasion, was assigned clean-up duty with the custodian. When he refused to help, he was given additional demerits and more detention. His own father described him to the principal as "worthless."

One day as the staff was going over "problem students," a new art teacher commented on the creativity in some of Fred's graffiti. After some snide laughter, the art teacher volunteered to take Fred on as a project. The teacher spent some time just getting to know Fred and listening to his issues without getting defensive or trying to change his behavior.

Since a big game was coming up, the teacher commented on Fred's creativity in "tagging" the last several banners the pep club had made (he actually destroyed them). The teacher then said he was now in a jam because he had run out of volunteers to do banners and posters. He asked Fred if he would be willing to help out.

You guessed it . . . Fred worked long and hard creating banners and posters, several of which were very creative. He also cooperated well with several volunteers who showed up to help.

More important, he became protective of the school and even volunteered to help with a clean-up project. Much of his acting-out behavior disappeared and his interest in school work increased . . . particularly in the art class taught by his "mentor" for which he signed up. Even Fred's dad viewed his son differently, asking him to create a poster for his workplace! Fred felt understood, accepted, and confident that he had something significant to contribute . . . so he began to take school and himself seriously.

School-Smart Parenting Tip:
Sometimes it's easier to tame a fanatic than to put life back into a corpse. Turn liabilities into assets when possible!

Homework, school assignments, and voluntary projects can provide opportunities for children to perceive themselves as significant, active participants in their own education. The value of these activities depends much on the role children play in planning and contributing, as well as on the support and feedback they receive from parents and teachers.

Some parents actually do their children's homework for them (in the mistaken belief that they will ensure that it is done right). They believe they will increase their children's self-esteem by helping them get better grades.

Tragically, they actually communicate that their children do not count in the process of their own education. They fuel self-doubt and a sense of insignificance. They teach children that looking good is better than taking the risk and responsibility of learning to do well.

The child's role is to show up for class and bring the right books home so Mom and Dad can do the homework right. Their own efforts are unnecessary, their contributions irrelevant. They are, in fact, insignificant, passive recipients of their education, rather than active contributors to it.

Educators are well aware of the effect that cooperative and collaborative learning can have on a child's perception of significance. Parents can encourage such collaboration in numerous ways at home. By approaching family meetings, chores, family outings, rituals and traditions, games, and other activities collaboratively, parents can help children learn cooperation, which in turn will reinforce each child's perception of him- or herself as a significant contributor.

▼

Chapter 6

Developing Strong Perceptions of Personal Influence

God . . . grant me the serenity to accept the things I cannot change,
the courage to change the things I can, and the wisdom to know
the difference.

—The Serenity Prayer

This strategy addresses a very powerful need, that of the perception of control or influence over one's life. This is the foundation of personal accountability.

When people see their lives as controlled by fate, luck, or circumstances, they are said to have an **external locus of control.** Such a position is characteristic of more dependent, less self-reliant individuals. People who see themselves as capable of influencing events and circumstances through their actions, choices, and such are said to have an **internal locus of control,** which is characteristic of independent, more self-reliant individuals.

When children understand that they can't always control what happens to them, but they can influence how they respond to what happens, they pay closer attention to their actions and choices. This encourages hope, optimism, and accountability.

When they believe, instead, that they have no influence over what happens in life, that what happens is just a throw of the dice, they usually conclude that it doesn't matter what they do or what choices they make. This results in pessimism, which results in a lack of accountability for their lives and actions.

Tom Peters and Robert Waterman relate a fascinating story in their bestselling book, *In Search of Excellence* (Warner Books). A large group of individuals was given a series of pencil-and-paper tasks involving complex puzzles and proofreading. In the background were loud distracting noises—such as a mimeograph machine running, several people speaking in foreign languages, someone banging on a typewriter, and street noise.

Half the group were supplied with a control switch through which they could turn off the distracting noise; the other half were not. As you might guess, the half with the control switch scored significantly higher on the tasks than did the half without the switch.

But here's the kicker: Not one member of the group that had the control switch actually used it. Although they knew they could use the control switch at any moment to shut out the distracting noise, not one decided to do so.

The group with the control switch scored significantly higher than the group without the switch. The perception that they could influence their environment, that they had the potential power to act in their own behalf enabled them to focus more carefully and confidently and do a better job.

Cultural influences such as the mass media, education, and government often contribute to our perceptions of life. Parenting and teaching styles such as permissiveness and strictness are also considered factors that influence children's perceptions.

The process of affirming people as significant, covered in chapter 5, "Developing Strong Perceptions of Personal Significance," increases people's sense of being influential by validating them for their efforts. The experiences with problem-solving gained during class meetings and family meetings (which will be further discussed in chapter 14, "Emotional Stability") also contribute to children's senses of influence.

A friend frequently says that if it weren't for bad luck, he'd have no luck at all. As you might guess, his life is in shambles. When you believe that life is a matter of luck, and that some people get the good luck and succeed, while others get the bad luck and do not, then you have a ready prescription for giving up at the first sign of misfortune.

Applications of this in schooling are numerous. When children see themselves as having influence over events in life, they will evaluate experiences and seek ways to increase the probability of positive outcomes. When they want to get better grades, they believe that studying harder can help that happen. When they want to be treated with kindness and respect, they have learned that it helps to do likewise with others.

If they want to avoid detentions or suspensions, they learn to be accountable for their behavior in class. In short, as children are encouraged to reflect on their experiences, both in and out of school, they learn to identify the kinds of actions and decisions that lead to results they prefer (rather than to results they do not care for). In this way, they develop an appreciation of influence.

What is the opposite of this perception? It is the third-grader who believes that all the other children are picking on him, the fifth-grader who complains that the tests are all too hard, the middle school student who is convinced that she gets in trouble because none of the teachers understand her.

How can we parents help our children avoid such thinking? Of the third-grader, we can ask, patiently and respectfully: "What things can you do to get along better with your classmates?" Of the fifth-grader: "What tricks have you learned to help you study better for the tests?" Of the middle school student: "What is one thing you can do to help just one of your teachers understand you better?"

Notice that in each case, we communicate that the solution to the problem lies within the child: "What things can *you* do . . . ?" "What tricks have *you* learned . . . ?" "What is one thing *you* can do . . . ?" Follow this up with empathic listening (providing counsel as needed), and steady progress will result. Parents often feel they must run to school to confront the teacher or principal with the responsibility of solving children's problems. This may be called for at times, but such occasions should be rare, and should only take place after we have done all we can to empower our children to do all they can to solve their own problems.

We do a disservice to children when we communicate a perception that everything is someone else's problem rather than theirs. "You are doing poorly in school because the teacher doesn't like you." "You didn't make the team because the coach is prejudiced." "Nobody likes you because you're different."

It is easy to reinforce such perceptions; it is more difficult to communicate to our children that problems are challenges we believe they can tackle successfully because they are capable and significant individuals who can influence the occurrences in their lives. The key to fostering a positive self-perception is sincere, empathic listening plus respectful redirecting of the child's thought processes, ("What can *you* do?") followed, when necessary, by mature counseling. Yes, such gentle guidance can be time-consuming in the short run; but it pays big dividends in the long run. Capable young people are certainly worth the effort.

The Power of Three

The perceptions of being capable, significant, and able to influence one's own life are powerful confidence-builders that instill the courage to take healthy risks, improvise, and transcend failure. Parents who invest time helping children internalize these perceptions are going a long way toward ensuring that their children will succeed in school and enjoy learning.

These three perceptions are critical to children's ability to be proactive in problem solving and learning through experience. Attitudes, motivation, and behavior stem from and are nurtured by perceptions. Confidence and effectiveness in performing the daily tasks and challenges of life are highly influenced by skills. As children's self-perceptions grow stronger, four sets of skills help complete their toolbox for effective living and learning.

▼

Chapter
7

Developing Strong Intrapersonal Skills

Emotional intelligence (EQ) has a much greater effect on success in life and learning than does intellectual quotient (IQ). . . .
—Daniel Goleman, *Emotional Intelligence*

This strategy, developing strong intrapersonal skills, helps build the foundation of emotional health and well-being. Every day of our lives we experience our own feelings and encounter the feelings of others—feelings that require our responses and the intrapersonal skill to respond appropriately.

Some families and cultures do not teach, model, or encourage healthy ways of dealing with emotional experiences. People raised in such confusion practice avoidance, denial, projection, or repression of feelings.

Intrapersonal skills, which include self-assessment, self-control, and self-discipline, can be developed through modeling, encouragement, and active teaching.

People who lack intrapersonal skills often have difficulty controlling impulses and acting appropriately on emotions. They often feel they have little or no control over their actions and find it difficult to set limits for themselves. They tend to believe that their actions and experiences are caused by events, feelings, and even other people.

The first skill we will discuss is self-assessment, which is the ability to recognize and describe one's feelings in first-person terms. For example: "I'm feeling angry!" "I'm upset about . . . !" or "I feel frustrated when . . . !" rather than "She makes me angry (upset, frustrated, and so on)."

We confuse children when we use or allow them to use projective language. Try to use **"I" statements** when describing your own feelings and help children do so as well! It is important that children realize they are entitled to their feelings and that experiencing and acknowledging them is not "wrong," "bad," or "inappropriate." Therefore, once feelings are acknowledged and accepted, we need to avoid judging ("You shouldn't feel that way!") or rationalizing them ("Why do you feel that way?"). Focusing on responses and results ("What did you do in response to the feeling?" and "What were the results of your doing that?") is far more helpful.

By asking questions such as these, we help children become aware that feelings do not make people do things—**people do things in response to feelings.** The ability to *act* rather than *react* in response to feelings is what we call self-control.

Once people learn to own their feelings and to accept responsibility for acting on them, they begin to develop self-discipline. Self-discipline is the ability to recognize one's feelings, identify a desired outcome, then adjust one's behavior appropriately.

To develop this skill, people need to be allowed to experience the results of various responses to feelings and then encouraged to consider the results of alternative responses without being judged or criticized for those results.

An emotionally immature person may see the event this way: "Sarah got me grounded!" and believe the other person caused the outcome. A person with intrapersonal skills would say: "When that event happened, I felt frustrated and dealt with my frustration by throwing some things around. As a result of handling my frustration that way, I'm on restriction. Next time I'm frustrated, I need to handle it differently, or I could set myself up for more of such difficulties!"

Michael has two friends, Bob and Jeri, who have been taking country and western dance lessons. The two commit to taking periodic lessons and going dancing at least twice a month. Frontline baby boomers, both are pushing fifty years old. But there is a big difference between them: While Bob looks like he's pushing fifty, Jeri could easily pass for ten years younger.

Their dance instructor is a tall, handsome, young cowboy who can two-step with the best of them. Bob has none of the above attributes. The dance instructor has taken a liking to Jeri, who is a natural dancer. So whenever he demonstrates a new step, he invites her to be his partner. They dance slow, they dance fast, they dance close, and they dance apart. Predictably, Bob gets jealous.

Now don't try to tell Bob that he has no right to get jealous. Don't try to tell him that he is being immature. He will tell you that he is jealous and that he will hold fast to his jealousy and no one will talk him out of it, thank you very much.

Given his feeling, over which he probably has little or no control, Bob has choices regarding how he responds to the jealousy. He could saunter up to the bar and check out some youngish cowgirl with "Louann" or "Brandy" or "Betty Sue" on the back of her belt and lead her to the dance floor . . . and make a complete fool of himself. He could invite Mr. Tall, Young, Handsome Two-Stepper outside for a less-than-friendly discussion . . . and make an even bigger fool of himself. He could retreat into himself and give Jeri the silent treatment all the way home. Or he could just be thankful that he is married to someone whom much younger men find attractive. The choice is his.

If Bob handles the above situation effectively, he will be modeling skill in self-assessment, self-control, and self-discipline. Self-assessment means acknowledging feelings uncritically and without apology. Self-control involves acting in response to those feelings. Self-discipline entails identifying the desired or acceptable outcome and then behaving accordingly.

We express these skills, called the *intra*personal skills because they are applied within us, in varying degrees of effectiveness on a daily basis. When we acknowledge our feelings or encourage others to acknowledge theirs without projecting their feelings onto others, we model self-assessment.

Parents who respond to a child's fear of the dark with "Don't be ridiculous; there's nothing to be afraid of!" are telling the child that he has no right to his feelings. A more helpful approach would be along the following lines:

> Dad: Son, it's time to turn the lights off and go to sleep.
>
> Robby: I can't, Dad; I'm afraid of the dark.
>
> Dad: Well, I can understand that, Robby. I remember being afraid of the dark myself when I was your age. What might you do to feel less afraid?
>
> Robby: I could sleep in your room.
>
> Dad: Yes, you could, but that wouldn't help you learn to get comfortable in your own room, would it? So what else could you do?
>
> Robby: Maybe if we leave the hall light on, it would help.

Dad: That's a great idea. Let's try that. Also, I'd like to tell you something that helped me when I was your age. When I could hear my parents' voices, I wasn't so afraid. Do you think that might help?

Robby: Sure. Could you talk to Mom so I can hear you and not be afraid?

What is Dad accomplishing? First of all, he encourages his son to acknowledge his fear. He does not try to talk him out of it, but instead validates the boy's feelings and communicates empathy.

Second, he focuses on actions his son can take in response to (rather than on) the fear itself. He helps his son problem-solve by demonstrating alternatives, some more attractive than others, thereby encouraging self-control.

Further, he shares with his son, in a helpful and supportive way, wisdom he accumulated from his own experiences in dealing with feelings. He helps his son develop self-discipline by helping him understand the difference between what he might *want* to do and what he *needs* to do in order to produce the **outcome** he desires (valuable insights to communicate to children!).

The applications of these skills in school are numerous. An important element for success in school is the work ethic. This requires mastery of the basic principle that some things in life need to be done whether we want to do them or not.

Perhaps in a perfect world, we could all do whatever we want, whenever we want. A school that attempts to replicate such a utopian world by not setting requirements for students does a disservice to them, because the "real" world does not work that way. The world our children will enter as citizens with responsibilities is a world of requirements and tasks that need to be done.

Any school that purports to teach "the basics" must include opportunities for students to develop self-discipline. Homework, individual and group projects, book reports, oral reports, independent learning activities, and portfolio assignments provide children with opportunities to develop skills in dealing with wants and needs. When parents support children's efforts and encourage them to learn from their choices, children acquire self-discipline.

Consider Jimmy, a very likable child in Michael's school who, nonetheless, had difficulty with self-control throughout his school experiences. A shove at the locker, a push in the cafeteria line, an unkind word, even a careless look could be occasion for Jimmy to explode in anger and lash out at a classmate.

For years Jimmy's teachers tried to control him, suggesting few if any alternatives to his exploding. By the time he was in sixth grade, Jimmy had gained little if any skill in dealing with his problems. He had also matured early and was now the biggest boy in the class, bigger even than his teacher. What would she do if Jimmy exploded and she could not restrain him or calm him down?

Anticipating possible problems on a scheduled field day (a day of much less structure and much more physical interaction than a regular school day), the teacher sent Jimmy to the office for counseling. In the past, Michael and other members of the staff had focused entirely on ways to get Jimmy to avoid angry feelings. They told him not to get angry just because a classmate called him a name. They encouraged him to ignore what others might say or do. All their suggestions had been to no avail.

This time they took a different approach. Michael asked Jimmy what he might do the next time he felt his anger rise. One option he thought he might try was to leave the situation and come to the office to talk. Because Jimmy often sought out one-on-one adult attention, and had a positive relationship with him, Michael felt confident enough to try this approach. Although Michael was aware that Jimmy might abuse the privilege from time to time because of his strong desire for one-on-one attention (for example . . . he might leave a class to avoid an unpleasant assignment), the risk was certainly worth it.

Jimmy never did abuse the privilege. During the next year, he came to the office maybe four times, each time in the heat of anger, on the very brink of exploding. But each time, as he felt his anger rising, he remembered that he had an alternative. He could withdraw temporarily from the situation, go somewhere else to cool off, and even enjoy that cooling off time—chatting about anything and everything with the principal of the school as his anger slowly subsided.

Thankfully, during his remaining two years, Jimmy didn't lose control, or even feel a need to visit the office. He did, however, stop by to visit Michael just to say hello whenever he got a chance. What Jimmy learned were the skills of self-assessment ("I am feeling angry") and self-control ("I can make choices when I feel angry, and what I choose to do will affect the outcome!").

When Jimmy's teachers stopped asking him why he was angry and focused instead on what he might do when he was angry, they encouraged him to shift from a *reactive* to a *proactive* mode, from "I am angry; therefore I hit" to "I am angry; what do I need to do about it?"

When we teach self-assessment and self-control at home, we help children deal more effectively with many situations they encounter at school. At home, they have perhaps one or two other children to deal with; at school, they typically have twenty-five or more. They will encounter a much wider range of feelings and emotions in their classmates than they do at home, and will experience a wider range of emotions themselves. They will meet adults who may or may not be as supportive as their parents have been—adults who may or may not accept their feelings, who may or may not be willing or able to work with them in making appropriate responses to feelings.

Parents can help their children develop these skills before and during their journeys through school. When we model self-assessment, self-control, and self-discipline in our own lives, and work patiently and supportively to help our children practice these skills, we gather tools for a lifetime of emotional wellness.

Chapter

8

Developing Strong Interpersonal Skills

Seek first to understand, then to be understood.

—Stephen Covey

Interpersonal (or "people") skills include these abilities: to **listen, communicate, cooperate, negotiate, share, and empathize.** We learn through experience how to do these; all are built on a foundation of dialogue.

Interpersonal skills are often inadequately developed in individuals. By **modeling** good listening, **practicing** meaningful dialogue, and **structuring** the environment to provide practice and reinforcement, we enable children to greatly improve their listening and other "people" skills.

Those without adequate interpersonal skills are left isolated and vulnerable. We call such people "high-risk individuals." Because high-risk individuals have inadequate skills in understanding and working with others, they are frequently unsuccessful in personal relationships. This void frequently leads to behaviors such as depression, excessive alcohol or drug use, or participation in activities that substitute but do not fulfill their need for effective relationships. Substance use/abuse, for example, often deludes people into feeling they are relating better to others, which can lead to increasing use of such substances as "social lubricants."

Skills that help one deal effectively with others decline for several reasons. One major deterrent in our society is excessive television viewing. Television detracts us from developing the skills to deal with others in two ways: First, it preempts other activities such as reading, thinking, and dialogue that promote communication, cooperation, negotiation, and such; secondly, it reinforces passive, non-developmental participation in one's world.

Compare TV with radio in which one has to visualize the hero, the villain, and all other aspects of the story. Upon hearing that the hero is hurt, children usually imagine a hero and come up with an image that fits their own values, attitudes, and perceptions. They also tend to imagine the kind of hurt (bleeding? falling down the mountain?) and often feel the hero's pain. Compare this experience with watching a depiction on television that portrays the hero according to someone else's reality. Even though the hero may not in any way reflect appropriate attitudes or acceptable behaviors, children are likely to be receptive to the values of the hero they see on the screen. They do not imagine the details; these are portrayed for them—in full color, often with instant replays.

However, before children can fully empathize with the character's plight, they are given the opportunity to forget the whole scene while being bombarded with deodorant, toothpaste, or cereal commercials. Again, television may preempt a child's opportunity to develop the ability to feel, think, process, or experience situations actively, at a personal level.

When television occurs in the context of greatly reduced dialogue with mature adults (due, for example, to loss of extended family, both parents working, or a single-parent family) and reduced dialogue in schools (due to large classes or short periods, for example), the total experience may be far below adequate.

Through listening skills, children learn to understand or empathize with others' feelings. They learn this as they experience others listening to and understanding them. As children are listened to, they learn to listen. **As children are understood, they learn to understand others.**

Many things hinder children's learning how to listen, and therefore how to communicate, cooperate, negotiate, and empathize. One major roadblock is what we have called "adultism"—that peculiar way of thinking adults have. Children see things from a different perspective than adults do.

It is important that we listen for a child's perceptions. Often, instead of listening, adults try to force their perceptions onto children—perhaps using threats, warnings, and negatives such as "That makes no sense!" or "What in the world made you think that?" Instead of helping children learn, such remarks make them feel threatened or believe their own perceptions are invalid and have no meaning.

When such "adultisms" continue to hang over them like clouds, children begin to clam up, become intimidated as learners, and wait until they can do exactly as told. This leads to more warnings, threats, and directions as the adult thinks the child is not listening or not obeying.

Another roadblock to bringing out children's perceptions is talking for them. "Did you, can you, do you, will you, won't you, are you, aren't you . . . ?" can all be answered with a grunt, harumph, or nothing. We come closer to the child's perception when we ask questions such as, "What were you trying to accomplish?" "What were the results of what you did?" "What ideas do you have?" "How does it look to you?"—with genuine interest in hearing the answers! These examples illustrate the difference between talking *to* or *for* people and talking *with* them. Below are twelve major roadblocks to effective communication that we call **The Dirty Dozen.** Helping children learn to recognize and avoid them is essential to their developing "people" skills.

THE DIRTY DOZEN

Showing Power
"Don't give me that!" "I don't want to hear it!"

Giving "You" Messages
"You always think that!" "You never . . . !"

Advising
"That shouldn't make any difference!" "You should just . . . !"

Lecturing
"I don't see any reason for . . . !" "I don't know why you can't just . . . !"

Judging
"That's a dumb idea!" "When will you ever learn?"

Praising
Nonspecific—"That's great!" "Good for you!"

Name Calling
"Look, stupid, . . . !" "You big chicken!" "Dummy!"

Ridiculing

"You're a fool if you do!" "How could you fall for that?"

Interpreting

"You're just feeling pressured!" "You can see how that . . . !"

Giving False Reassurance

"Everything will work out fine!" "I'm sure you won't mind!"

Attacking

"I'll teach you to say no to me!" "Just shut your mouth!"

Avoiding

"Now just don't get upset about it!" "Let's get off that subject!"

Michael's Experience with Dialogue

For years we have started each school day with announcements over the intercom, and for years I have invited individual students to join me in making the announcements. I also looked on this practice as an opportunity to spend a few quality moments with students before it was time to broadcast the announcements, to "get into their quality world," to know them individually.

What a disappointment it was! I would invite them to sit down, and as soon as they appeared to be comfortable, I would open with: "Well, how's it going?" or "How was your weekend?" or "What's new?" Their responses were predictable: "Fine." "Okay." "Nothin'."

What's wrong with kids today? I wondered. Can't they communicate? Aren't we teaching communication skills in this school?

So I decided it was time to put into practice some behaviors I was teaching in my parenting seminars. I planned to make a conscious effort to ask questions that would encourage students to give intelligent replies. I asked questions that could not be answered with a yes, a no, or a grunt.

Instead of "How was your weekend?" I tried: "Well, what was the best thing that happened for you over the weekend?" Instead of "What's new?" or "How's it going?" I switched to: "So, what's the most interesting thing going on for you right now?"

The result was immediate and significant change. My technique proved almost traumatic for some students. They would open their mouths, ready to respond with "Just fine," then they would stop—mouths still open, eyes wide—and look to the ceiling, as if for inspiration.

I could only guess what they were thinking: "He wants a real answer? He's not going to let me out of here until I respond! I can't get off with 'Just fine.' I'll have to take responsibility for what I think!"

Then their eyes would drop and, noting that I still waited patiently for an answer, they would respond: "Well, we won our soccer tournament yesterday." "My grandparents are coming to visit." "My mom told us she's going to have a baby." "I passed my spelling test."

For other students, those with highly developed interpersonal skills (a euphemism in the teaching trade for "likes to talk a lot"), my carefully phrased questions opened floodgates. No trauma here, just eager acceptance of the invitation to share feelings, thoughts, and wishes.

Sometimes I had to cut off the conversation lest the morning announcements never get made! But in either case, genuine conversation resulted. The students enjoyed the opportunity to share what was on their minds, and I got to know each student better. Not a bad outcome for such a minor change!

Try this experiment with your children. Instead of greeting them after school with "Did you have a good day?" switch to "What was the best or most important thing that happened today?" Instead of "Did you have fun at school today?" try "What did you do that was fun today?" Instead of "Did you learn anything new today?" try "What is one interesting thing you learned in school today?" or "What did you work on in science today?" (Or better yet, "Help me learn one thing you learned in school today.")

This simple shift in the way we ask questions can make the difference between receiving nondescript or intelligent, thought-out responses. But be patient: Just because *we* change does not automatically mean our children will respond to that change immediately.

The first time you ask, "What was the best thing that happened to you today?" they may very well respond with "Fine." Or they may say nothing, wondering what your hidden agenda is or why you started reading that stupid parenting book!

Keep at it patiently. Most important of all, sincerely and patiently listen when they do respond. Then be sure you pick up the conversation from their response, not from your own agenda. By doing so, you encourage communication and model respect. Children will usually become more conscious of what is happening at school when they believe you are eager to listen actively to their thoughts and experiences.

▼

Chapter

9

Developing Strong Systemic Skills

Learning to read situations and people accurately and adapting behavior accordingly are two of the most essential skills we can develop!

—H. Stephen Glenn, *Developing Capable People*

Every day of our lives each of us interacts with systems— the environment, traffic, family, the workplace, school, society. In systems, elements are interrelated so that there are consequences to every action taken. The skills one needs to deal with systems are responsibility (the ability to *respond* to limits and consequences), adaptability (the ability to *adopt different behaviors* in different settings and situations), and flexibility (the ability to *accommodate* others' needs and unexpected changes in one's plans).

To develop skills, people need a safe climate in which to risk learning, challenges that require their practicing the desired behavior, and reinforcement in the form of encouragement rather than reward(s). Once safety, challenge, and reinforcement are present in the environment, experience becomes the best teacher and patience is usually rewarded.

Two main environment types limit the development of responsibility. One is the permissive environment, in which limits are not established, or are not enforced, preventing children from learning how to work within them. Everything is usually negotiable *after the fact* and resolved in favor of good feelings. When such children are introduced to a structured situation such as school (a situation with many inherent limits), they generally are incapable of effective behavior because they cannot anticipate what will happen should they not follow the rules. They view control as people "being mean" or not caring about them.

Parents, teachers, and others tend to adopt permissiveness as a strategy in dealing with young people for three main reasons:

1. Excessive **need for approval** from the child or student
2. Fear or insecurity in the face of **conflict**
3. Lack of understanding about teaching through **consequences**

Another type of environment that limits children's development of responsibility is that in which parents adhere to an overly strict or coercive model; they make decisions arbitrarily and force their children to comply . . . or else! In many homes, excessive control is exerted through threats, warnings, punishment, and manipulation, all of which result in hostility, aggression, rebellion, and irresponsibility.

Many adults react quickly and angrily to situations in which a child makes a poor decision. **It is easier to impose control than to teach self-control!** By imposing control externally, these parents foster weakness, dependency, anger, and frustration.

When such directing or controlling takes the place of teaching, or when parents prevent their children from experiencing the results of behaviors or actions, they encourage irresponsibility. Unfortunately, this climate is typical of many homes and schools today. Teaching requires time, planning, and patience, but the results last longer because they provide direction and build the foundation for a value system that emphasizes personal responsibility.

The word discipline comes from the root word "disciple" which means "a student or follower of a principle." Discipline, then, is the willingness and ability to govern one's own behavior with respect to wants and needs, cause and effect, based on the principle of personal accountability.

Basically, five elements are essential in teaching systemic skills: unqualified positive regard; clear feedback about behaviors; a structure of results or consequences; firmness in following through; and a teaching process of exploring, with dignity and respect, what was learned from experience.

Unqualified positive regard means that a person's worth is not gained or lost through performance. When children can honestly acknowledge mistakes and errors without fear that we will think less of them, they experience a safe climate for learning.

Clear feedback separates the act from the actor so that we can talk about issues and specifics without creating defensiveness and resistance. The stairway to understanding (below) serves as a useful guide in giving effective feedback.

I feel _____

    about_____

      because_____

For example: I feel good about this test grade because it reflects the effort you put into it.

Experiencing results or consequences means allowing children to experience cause and effect (in the case of *natural* results) or (in the case of logical results) working to help them see that what is being required is *Related, Respectful, Reasonable,* and *Revealed* so they can use this information in their decision making and begin to accept responsibility for what they experience. This also forces us to be thoughtful so that we, too, are more likely to follow through if necessary.

Firmness in following through means that we honor the contracts we make. We do not renegotiate after the fact, nor do we seek revenge or punishment. We do not manipulate or change the outcome. We respect a person's right to experience the natural consequences or results of his or her actions and choices.

Teaching with dignity and respect means we do not add insult to injury by being critical, judgmental, or blaming. We avoid lecturing, explaining, and moralizing; instead, we patiently help the child explore what he or she learned from the experience (once emotions have stabilized) by asking: "What did you *experience* in the situation?" "What action(s) or choice(s) on your part contributed to (or *caused*) the outcome?" "What did you *learn* from this experience?" "How will knowing this *influence* what you do in the future?"

This approach reduces identifying with failure, emphasizes learning to do better, and teaches problem solving. It teaches children how to build on success and reduce the probability of repeating errors. The following chart provides a useful outline reminder of these five **Principles for Developing Responsibility.**

PRINCIPLES FOR DEVELOPING RESPONSIBILITY

1. Unqualified Love, Care, or Respect
Positive regard for people is not won or lost, earned or forfeited, based on what they do.

2. **Clear Feedback About Behavior**
Feedback is specific and related to the behavior rather than a judgment of the person.

3. **Experience Results**
The outcome follows the action whenever possible so that cause and effect is revealed to the person.

4. **Firmness**
Those in authority say what they mean and mean what they say, so that they can be trusted to follow through.

5. **Teaching With Dignity and Respect**
The emphasis is placed on bringing out what was learned from the experience rather than on the event itself.

In developing systemic skills in young people, it is important to help them learn the relationship between adaptability and responsibility. For many people, this requires making a major paradigm shift from adult-imposed, reactive, manipulative control to proactive empowerment achieved with the young person.

Are dads and moms always on the same page when it comes to expectations for children? Are discipline standards always the same? Are discipline *practices* always the same? Do the very same things annoy each parent, and do they agree all the time on what small matters can be ignored and what large matters demand attention? Of course not.

The same goes for teachers. Teachers come from widely varying backgrounds and experiences and have value systems that may or may not parallel those of the majority of their students. Some teachers more often than not will be too strict; others will more often than not be too permissive.

The most effective teachers approach a level of consistency that varies only occasionally. The best schools practice a philosophy of discipline and standards that all their teachers buy into and, with few exceptions, practice. But individual differences will always remain, and students need to be able to accept and adapt to those differences.

Responsibility, which on the most basic level is the ability to anticipate the consequences of one's actions in a given situation and to choose an appropriate response from various options rather than just react, is the natural outcome of adaptability and flexibility. In addition to following the process discussed above, we can help children learn these skills by the way we respond to their complaints about school, as the following dialogue demonstrates:

> Catherine: This school is so stupid. The math teacher gives us detentions if we forget to raise our hands, and the social studies teacher lets us do anything we want! Why can't they get their act together?
> Dad: That can be frustrating. I can remember having teachers like that. It's hard to remember how to act sometimes.
> Catherine: I know. I got a detention from the math teacher and it's the school's fault!
> Dad: Well, we probably can't change the way your teachers handle discipline, although I can understand why you might want to. So what can you do to avoid getting into trouble in math class again?
> Catherine: Maybe I'll write in huge letters across my math book, 'Catherine, you are in math class now. Remember that you're not allowed to breathe for the next 50 minutes!'
> Dad: Great idea! And on your social studies notebook, why don't you write 'Catherine, breathe the sweet air of freedom!' Let me know how your plan works.

Empathy, a little humor, and a lesson in adaptability— all lead to a more responsible student. Notice that Dad felt no need to criticize his daughter for her negative attitude. No need to pontificate about responsibility. No need to play the role of the authoritarian parent. Just offer a little empathy and respect.

In the above dialogue, Dad modeled flexibility, adaptability, and responsibility by helping Catherine identify her alternatives and see which alternatives are more effective in which settings, then redirecting accountability back to her in a respectful and nonjudgmental manner. Catherine is much more likely to internalize flexibility, adaptability, and responsibility because Dad worked through her frustration *with* her rather than going into a lecture mode, telling her what she did wrong, why she did it wrong, and what she needs to do to fix it.

▼

Chapter

10

Developing Strong Judgment Skills

Decision making is to respond to the immediate issues of a
situation. . . . Judgment is to bring in higher order considerations.
　　　　　　　　　—U.S. Air Force Pilot Training Manual

Judgment, the most abstract and uniquely human of the
seven essential resources, is supported by development
in the other six areas. **Mature human judgment is an**
acquired characteristic that is heavily influenced by psychological development and learning.

　Children enter the world with no real knowledge of
themselves or others. In early childhood, they are almost
totally dependent on environmental stimulation to teach
them the principles and concepts that apply to the choices
they make. Children do not think like adults. In fact, children differ in their way of thinking according to the level
of cognitive development they have achieved.

　It is helpful for parents to study the process of cognitive development and learn what is reasonable to expect

of children at different stages. While such discussion is beyond the scope of this book, we would like to offer the following chart **(Stages of Cognitive Development)** as an oversimplified but helpful reference.

STAGES OF COGNITIVE DEVELOPMENT		
Age	Stage	Judgment Types/Principles
0–2	Sensorimotor	World of here and now Pain—Pleasure Can—Can't
2–6	Preoperational	Sees only one aspect at a time Thinking is rigid Either/or Safe—Dangerous Good—Bad
6–11	Concrete	Begins to understand abstract relationships Able to use logical thought when solving problems involving concrete objects, events, and ideas such as Cause—Effect Legal—Illegal "What will happen if_____?"
11+	Abstract/ Conventional	Capable of dealing with hypothetical concepts Discriminates between abstract concepts Appropriate/Inappropriate Fair/Unfair "How might_____feel about_____?"

(It should be noted that these stages, identified by Jean Piaget, represent normal possibilities for age ranges. Individuals may vary considerably based on personal factors and the developmental stimulation of their environment.)

Given their levels of readiness, how can we help children learn to make effective, appropriate, and ethical judgments that take into account not only their own wants and needs but those of others as well? How can we prepare them to make "sound judgments" rather than "poor judgments" in their school experiences?

Children acquire such wisdom and judgment skills when they are given opportunities to gain experience and explore concepts, principles, and relationships as they encounter them. Much of the groundwork for judgment is laid prior to the child's becoming an adolescent. This is extremely important in understanding the difficulties that teenagers who have not previously developed judgmental skills have in learning concepts, developing principles, and building relationships.

In order to make a judgment, a person must be able to go into new situations and determine (1) *What* is significant? (2) *Why* is it significant? (3) *How* does it affect my behavioral options or choices?

Applying the principle of teaching through exploring the "What?" "Why?" and "How?" of experiences provides training in finding meaning in one's experience as well as a foundation for decision making and problem solving. Therefore, we need to help children learn to ask these questions for themselves. As they experience success in questioning themselves, we teach them to do what we have been doing for them.

When we give feedback about positive and negative behavior, as outlined in the previous lesson on responsibility ("I feel . . . about . . . because . . ."), we share our perceptions and criteria with children. We help them see what we see in a less threatening and more encouraging manner.

On the other hand, using "adultisms"—expecting or demanding that children see or understand what we see without teaching or encouraging—actually works against their developing mature judgment. The child is threatened, often feels inadequate, and frequently seeks to escape or avoid mature adults rather than to identify with them and see things as they do.

When we avoid adultisms and focus on the child's perceptions and understanding of events and experience, we encourage learning. When we share our perceptions, criteria, and experience with others in nonjudgmental and nonthreatening ways, we encourage children to view experiences more maturely.

This question leads us directly to the sensitive topic of classroom behavior. A child's behavior in the classroom used to be an uncomplicated affair. If a child acted up, the teacher responded quickly and forcefully; so too would the parents. And, not long ago, so too did the neighbors! If Mrs. Campbell, who lived on the corner and knew everything going on in the neighborhood (particularly, it seemed, what the Brock boys were up to), caught Michael throwing snowballs at cars on the way home from school, Michael's mother would know about it before he reached home. And Mom would thank Mrs. Campbell for the information.

For better or worse, that scenario has changed. It may take a whole village to raise a child, but today's villages have become too fragmented and polarized to rise to that important challenge.

So the issue of classroom behavior has become more sensitive, and more difficult for today's teachers to handle. As parents, we would do well to ask ourselves, frankly and honestly, how we want children to behave in the classroom. Do we want them to behave as if the entire world revolves around their every want and need? Do we want them to be class clowns? Do we want them to be disruptive? Or do we, instead, want them to be respectful of others?

Respect is fundamental to everything we do in life. This principle holds the key to resolving many of the world's ills, from family problems to global crises. Unfortunately, respect is a word that is frequently used without understanding of its underlying principle.

Many of us grew up hearing that we were supposed to respect our elders. Most likely, we were taught that the mother is supposed to respect the father and the children are supposed to respect the parents. If you were in the military, you were taught to respect the higher rank. All that is fine as far as it goes; unfortunately, it doesn't go far.

Respect is not a one-directional virtue. It is not meant to flow exclusively in a vertical path, from "lower" to "higher." Nor is it something that is deserved by "higher" and earned by "lower." It is, on the other hand, something that belongs to every living thing and is held in trust by all human beings. It belongs to the wife as well as to the husband; it belongs to the son as well as to the father. In short, respect is not earned; it is held in trust for and by all human beings.

Some of the saddest relationships we have encountered while working with parents and children over the years are relationships dependent on rank. Such relationships often reflect failure to understand that the structure of military relationships does not translate well to the family. In such home environments, the relationship between the father and the children—and sometimes between the father and the mother—is not one of love, but one of power or rank. The children are taught that they must respect those who outrank them. The idea of respect as a correlative of love is nonexistent. And there is absolutely no understanding of respect being owed or given. "You want my respect; you'll have to earn it."

One way we teach respect is by modeling it. We can show respect for children and encourage them to respect others, *all* others—older and younger, richer and poorer, of every race, color, and belief. That may be simple to understand, but is not always easy to do. When we speak to children as people of dignity, we teach them respect. When children see us deal respectfully with all the people with whom we come in contact—our neighbors, salespeople, the secretary at the office, the workers who come to our homes—they learn what respect is in reality.

Follow this up by using dialogue to explore *what* the children observe in your behavior, *why* they believe it is important to deal with people in such ways, and *how* they see themselves behaving toward others in ways that show respect. Whenever possible, create opportunities to involve them in role-taking situations. For example: "If you were in my situation and had to _____, what would you need to consider in coming up with the most respectful way to handle it?"

Such role-playing will help prepare them to make necessary judgments about how to treat others—friends, strangers, classmates, students, and teachers—with respect. It will also help them know that they, too, are worthy of respect by virtue of their humanity.

> ### School-Smart Parenting Tip:
> **Share your beliefs about a moral or ethical principle with children in an open, non-judgmental way, then model the principle in interactions with people. "There is no better way to reach respect than to model it!"**

When we add concerted effort to work with children in problem solving and decision making to the modeling of principles, we will further reinforce effective and appropriate judgment skills. Some opportunities require awareness and commitment . . . but the results are definitely worth the effort!

The Process

We can create a structure with respectful limits on what children can do, then clarify these boundaries by sharing with our children what we considered when setting them. We can then allow children to make their own choices within our limits, and support them as they choose. (Remember that it is safest for them to make poor choices when they are younger!) When a child makes a poor choice (focus on the choice or the outcome rather than the child!), we can help him or her evaluate the process of choosing. By teaching children to look for solutions rather than blame, and to celebrate what they learn from the experience, we help them develop effective judgment skills.

A way to summarize the process of teaching judgment might be:

1. **Resist telling** children what the most appropriate response to a situation would be.
2. Instead, **ask** them what they see as possible responses.
3. Then, through questioning, **encourage their evaluation** of the possibilities based on criteria that reflect their beliefs.
4. Raise questions (when necessary) that **reflect stored wisdom** from your wider range of experiences.
5. **Support them in practicing** judgment skills by exploring results—both positive and negative—to see what they learned from the experience that would influence future decisions.

Recently, Steve and his son Mike were entering a shoe store. A mother just ahead of them told her son, "You can choose the pair you want!" The little boy ran off and soon came back with a pair of $150 big-name sport shoes. The mother grabbed them and exclaimed, "I didn't mean those!" She then walked to a sale table and told him to "Pick out a pair of basic tennis shoes." When he picked up a pair, she said, "The soles on those will come loose!" then picked up an ugly pair of "sturdy" shoes and said, "Here, take these!"

Mike whispered to Steve, "He won't like wearing them, Dad! She told him he could choose then wouldn't let him have what he wanted." The mother's intention was good, but the execution left a lot to be desired. A better approach would have been: "I have budgeted $____ for some tennis shoes. You can choose the pair that you want up to that price . . . but whatever you choose will have to get you by for the next four months." Then allow the boy to choose!

If he chooses poorly and the sole comes loose in a couple of months . . . show him how to use duct tape so he can get by until time for a new pair. Then, when it's time to buy new shoes, discuss what he learned: "What happened with the last shoes? Why did that happen? How will that experience influence your choice this time?"

Remember, life seldom presents clear-cut right and wrong choices . . . most of the time several responses to a situation are possible. The trick is to take your best shot and learn from the outcome how to make better decisions next time. As a recent Frank and Ernest cartoon said, "The problem is, school is mostly about true or false, while life is all essay questions!"

The strategies in this section of the book provide a blueprint for the capable student. Developing strength in The Significant Seven will set a foundation for effective living and learning . . . whether the learning takes place at school or elsewhere in life. Part Two, "The Capable Family," presents strategies for creating and maintaining a home environment that nurtures these resources on an ongoing basis.

▼

Part
___
II

The Capable Family

"So just what are the most important things our family can do to ensure that my child's school years will be happy and successful?"

That question, raised every year by parents who are approaching their child's first school experience, takes center stage in this second part of our look at developing capable students. The answer lies in focusing on parenting and providing a supportive home environment. But how is that accomplished?

In chapter 11, "The Most Important Thing," we identify what we most need to do to support our children's education. In chapters 12, "A Family of Contributors"; 13, "An Affirming Family"; and 14, "Emotional Stability," we identify and explore ways to create a home environment characterized by contribution, affirmation, and emotional stability. And in chapter 15, "Walking the Talk—Modeling," we stress the importance of walking the talk—role modeling—to help our children develop as capable students.

▼

Chapter

11

The Most
Important Thing

Who am I? I am my kid's mom!

—Dr. Laura Schlessinger

Syndicated talk show host and bestselling author Dr. Laura Schlessinger likes to open her radio show by introducing her engineer, her producer, her call screener, and finally herself, with what has become her signature opening: "And me? I am my kid's mom." Of all the parts that make up Dr. Laura, of all the roles she plays in life, Mom is the identity she uses to introduce herself to a national radio audience: "I am my kid's mom."

With that opening, Dr. Laura answers questions that are asked frequently during parent conferences and at parenting presentations and workshops: "What is the most important thing we can do to help our child have a successful school experience?" "How can I raise my child to be a capable student?" "What can I do to most effectively support my child's education?" The best answer? Just learn to be effective as your kids' mom . . . or your kids' dad.

Joey

When Joey started school, his dad, a teacher, decided to assume the full responsibility for his son's education. Everything Joey would learn in life would come from Dad. Joey became Dad's little project, through which he could justify his own worthiness to the world.

And so it came to be. Joey brought his homework to Dad, who sat by his side telling him the correct way to do it. When Joey protested that Dad's method was not the way the teacher taught him, Dad assured him that he knew best. After all, he was a teacher, too.

As Joey progressed through the grades and entered sports, his dad became a coach and decided he would assume full responsibility for his son's athletic development. Whenever possible, Dad took over the coaching position so he could direct his son every step of the way. When this was not possible, Dad would re-teach Joey, showing him the real way to kick the ball or hold the bat. Again, when Joey protested that that was not the way the coach had taught him, Dad assured him that he knew best. Was he not, after all, a coach as well?

When Joey reached the third grade, the first signs of discipline problems surfaced—what appeared to be a conscious tuning out of the teachers, an intentional refusal to accept their instruction. Considering what had been occurring for the past four years, this was no surprise. Joey was probably thinking: Why pay attention to the teachers at school when Dad is going to explain it all to me when I get home?

But soon the tuning out turned to overt disrespect. Joey demonstrated this lack of respectfulness not only toward the teachers, but to any adults—cafeteria workers, recess moderators, library personnel, coaches, and so on. Dad blamed the school: School wasn't meeting Joey's needs; it wasn't challenging him enough.

When Joey reached the fifth grade, Dad decided that he needed to be placed in a more challenging school. Joey resented being taken away from his friends; but, of course, Dad knew best.

Although the new school, a private school for the gifted, was more challenging, Joey's discipline problems only got worse. The disrespect toward adults increased, and an attitude of disrespect for his peers became evident as well. He was removed from games by referees, and removed from classrooms by teachers. By the end of the sixth grade, the new school had had enough of Joey. He was dismissed.

In desperation, Joey's parents called the principal of the old school and asked if he would give Joey a new chance. Joey got his chance, but only lasted a year. Disappointed with his continuing lack of progress and worsening discipline problems, his parents enrolled him in a school for students with motivation problems—his third school in three years. And throughout it all, Dad insisted on being Joey's teacher and coach.

Dad had made a major mistake—one that, tragically, he would never fully understand. Instead of being a parent to Joey, he became his teacher and coach. Joey didn't need a teacher and coach; he needed a dad. And so he rebelled.

This is an extreme case, but a true one. Parents have just one important role to play regarding children: to be effective as parents. Although we will have plenty of opportunities to support and guide children in their schooling, we do not need to be their formal classroom instructors. And although we will have numerous opportunities to coach them through the many school challenges they will face, we do not need to assume responsibility for the totality of their athletic development. We need to be their parents.

Temptation

The temptation to try to be *more* than our kids' mom or our kids' dad is a strong one. Whether, for example, we fear letting go, feel guilt for not doing all we think we should be doing, distrust the school system, or recall our own negative school experiences, many of us feel a need to take a far more active role in our children's education than our own parents took in ours.

The desire is wonderful, and the involvement can indeed make a great difference. The question is: "What form should our involvement take?"

Interestingly enough, many school personnel have come to believe, in response to societal changes, that the school should be taking a more active role in children's lives than just teaching the "three R's." In some school systems, the teaching role has expanded to cover areas previously reserved for parents.

Continuing public debate over such issues as sex education, character and values education, and health and HIV education represents much larger questions: What is the role of the parent? What is the role of the teacher? What is the role of the school system? What is the responsibility of the community? These larger issues will continue to play out in the fabric of society for years to come; it is not our purpose to resolve them here. The issue over which we have the most influence is our involvement as parents in the educational process.

A Parent's Perspective on Teaching

What is the role of the teacher? One response would be that the teacher's role is best defined in terms of the legal expression *in locus parentis*. No, the phrase doesn't have anything to do with the way our children make us feel, nor is it a condition that comes over us during the second or third week of summer. It's Latin for "in the place of the parents," and it suggests that the teacher's role is to take the place of the child's parents during the school day.

Why, you may ask, do parents need someone to take their place when it comes to the formal education of children? Why can't we take care of the teaching ourselves? Why do we need teachers to do it for us? Is it that we don't have enough time? Is it not a high enough priority for us? Is it because we lack expertise? These considerations are perhaps legitimate concerns for many. But, even when we have the time, the desire, and the expertise, at times parents are better off *not* being their children's formal teachers.

Why? Isn't it often said that parents are children's first teachers? Yes, it is . . . and yes, we are. But what does that mean? Does being our child's first teacher mean that it is primarily our job to teach our child the alphabet, the numbers, and how to write his or her name? Or that we are responsible to explain government and the workings of photosynthesis? Or does it mean instead that parents, by virtue of *being* parents, will be their children's teachers in the course of the daily experiences of life? An important key lies in the phrase *in the course of everyday life experiences.*

Parents As Teachers

In the course of the everyday experiences of life, parents do in fact teach. We teach values through our modeling and through our cautioning. Through our interactions with other adults and children—shopping, working, visiting at family and neighborhood gatherings, attending our place of worship—we teach interpersonal skills.

We teach sensitivity or insensitivity, tolerance or intolerance, patience or impatience, self-discipline or impulsiveness, empathy or judgmentalism, and a vast array of emotions and life skills through what we model and encourage in our children as we face life's daily challenges. We teach organization skills by our actions and when we encourage children's desire to collect and sort things, help them learn to clean their rooms and put away their toys, and involve them in household chores.

We teach grammar, again through our modeling and exhortation. Michael's mother, for example, worked heroically to teach him to say "I saw it" instead of "I seen it." Once she even had him repeat "I saw it" one thousand times. (To this day he still takes pleasure in getting a rise out of her by saying "I seen it!")

We can teach math while cooking, preparing meals, and setting the dinner table ("Please measure a half-cup of milk for me." "How many knives, forks, and spoons will we need?"), while shopping at the grocery store ("This is a small orange. Pick out three that are larger."), and while paying the bills ("How much will we have left in the account if we buy that soccer ball?").

We can teach history and geography while conversing about our own family heritage, walking through our neighborhood, and traveling around our country. If American history is little more than the study of immigration, as President Kennedy suggested in one of his more famous quotes, then how could that be explained better than through discussions of our own family history? We can teach by sharing stories of how our ancestors left their homelands (whether yesterday or a thousand years ago), why they came to America, where they first settled, where they migrated, and how they contributed.

No classroom lesson on mountains and valleys, cities and countrysides, oceans and deserts, or forests and plains can compete with the knowledge children gain while driving across America. (As Michael said, "Nothing I learned about mountains and valleys in elementary school prepared me for my first experience driving over the Rockies!")

We can help children become open to the wonderful world of science by taking advantage of what we come into contact with on a daily basis. We can teach them astronomy and earth science by talking about the sun and the moon, the stars and the planets, the seasons of the year, and the rocks and stones they pick up, climb over, and scrape their knees on.

We teach biology when we answer their many questions about animals and plants they see in the neighborhood or in the zoo. We encourage them to discover basic principles of science on their own by avoiding our temptation to fill their rooms with the latest toys advertised on television and instead provide them with resources of creative play—empty boxes, blocks, geometric shapes (cubes, spheres, inclined planes, arches, pillars, and so on), string, clay, and paper.

We help children broaden their horizons, expand their awareness of their world; provide further opportunities for their natural curiosity; and open their minds to a more ready acceptance of what they will learn in school when we take them to libraries, museums, live performances, parks, historical monuments, and different natural environments. We enhance their "cultural literacy" (a critical factor in developing reading skills, according to E. D. Hirsch, bestselling author of *Cultural Literacy: What Every American Needs to Know* [Vintage Books]) when we read them stories about the men and women, places and events, music and arts, and myths and legends that comprise the American experience.

We can teach the names of things we encounter in the world. We can teach table manners and communication skills. In short, we teach continuously, naturally, and informally—*in the course of our daily activities together.* We teach without a formal classroom, without a standard curriculum, and without formal teaching aids. (And, interestingly, even without special television or videotaped learning programs, "educational toys," or trips to theme parks.) **Our teaching flows naturally from our parenting.** The more natural it is, the more successful it will be.

Classrooms and Learning

Classroom educators, on the other hand, teach in a formal setting, with curriculum guides that outline minimum competencies, in an environment that could be described as "unnatural." What could be more unnatural than learning in artificial time segments with age as the primary grouping determinant? Do we parents teach manners between, say, 9:30 and 10:15 only? Do you know any families where all the children are the same age? And where there are twenty-five of them?

But that is schooling as we know it; and, frankly, this artificial setting appears to work rather well for the majority of students. Many teachers effectively teach spelling, sentence construction, division of fractions, and the causes of the Civil War. Across America, children learn biology, civics, phonics, and the difference between similes and metaphors in those unnatural settings we call schools. Could it be that essential learning does in fact occur more effectively in such structured settings? It appears so. Perhaps something about the very formality and structure and "unnaturalness" of school creates an environment conducive to learning about things that are not clearly relevant to the learner at the moment.

While the old complaint about schools not making content relevant to the student may well be true, that is beside the point: Much of what we learn is not clearly relevant to our present . . . but may be critical to our future, or critical to learning something else that *is* clearly relevant. The formality, structure, and unnaturalness of schooling may make learning those things more effective than otherwise.

A case in point might be a class lesson on the Bill of Rights. Can you imagine trying to teach the Bill of Rights through the course of your daily parenting? "While you're cutting that apple into four parts, dear, I am reminded of the third amendment proscription against the quartering of soldiers . . ." Well, maybe not! But we might agree that children should be well versed in the cornerstone of our rights, and should achieve a degree of literacy in understanding them so that they appreciate what we, soon-to-be-twenty-first-century Americans, have inherited and must preserve. A formal classroom setting in which students have the opportunity to experience and explore government issues appears to be most conducive to that learning.

Given all the above, how can we answer the initial question: "What is the best thing we can do to help our children succeed in school?" Again, the answer is both simple and difficult—simple in understanding, but difficult in practice: Be the most effective parent you can be in cultivating desire for and enjoyment of learning. Focus on the naturalness of teaching through parenting, not the unnaturalness of formal teaching.

Parents do not need to be children's formal classroom teachers. We do not need to explain the differences between islands and peninsulas, vowels and consonants, nouns and verbs (unless, of course, these things come up naturally in the course of our daily activities together).

School-Smart Parenting Tip:
Be alert for and create opportunities
to involve children in learning as a
spontaneous part of everyday activities.

We do not need to mortgage our homes to purchase the latest educational toys. Our children will not suffer serious harm if we cannot provide ready access to the Internet during their preschool years. They may, in fact, gain far more by using their imaginations to create games and activities, or by playing with crayons, cardboard boxes, blocks of wood, lumps of clay, piles of sand, or whatever!

Reading Readiness

Parents do not need to formally teach children to read. Read to your children, yes, but don't worry about *teaching* them to read. Give them your one-on-one attention, your closeness, your warmth, and read them the stories you have come to love. Whenever possible, involve them in the storytelling and cultivate their imagination and "ear" for language. **Dialogue and active imagination serve as critical foundations of reading readiness!**

Let them experience your excitement about and love for reading. Let them hear the sound of your voice as it rises and falls, as it expresses the fear and joy and sadness and determination that convey a full range of emotions, which will enhance your child's emotional growth. Let them develop their imaginations, explore their fantasies, confront their fears, all while nestled safely in the arms of a family member.

Make reading time one of your most nurturing parenting moments. Do it often. Make it a daily ritual. When they start their school years, they will see reading as a familiar and comfortable experience, one that they have come to associate with nurturing, warmth, personal attention, and positive family experiences. But don't worry about teaching them to read. Teachers can take care of that once the desire is there.

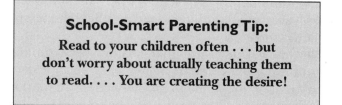

School-Smart Parenting Tip:
Read to your children often . . . but
don't worry about actually teaching them
to read. . . . You are creating the desire!

As children progress through their school years, learn when and how to relax. It is *not* always necessary to closely monitor their daily progress as they learn the various skills of reading, writing, and arithmetic. It is *not* always helpful to stand over them while they do homework (or, as is becoming more and more common, to do their homework for them). Since they need to design their own science projects, we can give up that responsibility, and relax . . . somewhat! Since schooling is *their* responsibility, we can use the seven strategies to help them meet the challenges.

So simply be the most effective parent you can be. Teach through the real-life situations, the everyday conversations, the spontaneous parenting moments, the modeling that occurs naturally in the course of your daily activities together. Create a home environment that maximizes the potential for natural real-life situations to turn into positive parenting moments. Learn and teach through them.

None of this is meant to suggest that a wall of separation should be erected between ourselves and children's schooling. Far from it! As parents, we are called upon to show real interest in our children's worlds, including their schooling.

We will no doubt find it appropriate from time to time to offer appropriate assistance and support with homework and school projects. When we do so, we will be most effective in our efforts to prepare children to experience success and happiness in school when we mentor them by exploring, guiding, and coaching rather than rescuing, directing, and explaining.

Beyond teaching through the natural opportunities of life and using the seven strategies, what specifically can we be doing in the home to most effectively support children in experiencing success and happiness in school? What specific attitudes and values can we cultivate? What specific behaviors can we strive to model?

Three Assets of Highly Effective Families

Through our many years of working with students and their families, we identified three areas in which family experience appears to maximize a child's potential for experiencing success and happiness in school. Although abundant research from various sources supports these assets, none we are aware of identifies them specifically as we present them. We offer our descriptions and suggestions based on our observations of their effectiveness over the years, not on the support of research.

Three assets of highly effective families are **contribution, affirmation,** and **emotional stability.** These characteristics support the Seven Strategies introduced in the previous chapters, greatly enhance the family experience for all involved, and have a direct impact on the school experience. They clearly indicate what parents and families can do to ensure an effective learning environment.

Our experience demonstrates that children raised in a home in which family members participate in chores come to school more willing and eager to assume their school responsibilities. They are more likely to take an active part in their own education. Children without the experience of actively contributing to the family process tend to expect that things be done for them; these students struggle with the concept of work, with doing things for themselves.

Children raised in homes in which their personal interests and talents are affirmed and supported tend to come to school eager to develop those interests and talents. They tend to be open to new interests and talents. On the other hand, children who have not experienced such affirmation tend to be resentful of and uncomfortable with the "script" their parents have written for them. Either they become overly compliant, passive recipients of learning (more of the same script), or rebels who reject school.

Children raised in a home characterized by emotional stability and support usually come to school happy, receptive, and eager to participate in this new community called a classroom. Children from emotionally unstable homes often arrive at school anticipating stress, insecurity, and negative communication, often creating such conditions in order to feel "normal."

Will these three family assets guarantee straight "A's" on the report card? Will they necessarily result in placement on the Honor Roll? Will they ensure acceptance into an Ivy League university? Probably not! These assets will, however, create an environment that encourages children to participate in school with a spirit of cooperation, a sense of appreciation and respect for individual differences, and a predisposition for problem solving through communication. These resources have been shown to have a greater impact on effectiveness in school than does native intelligence (IQ). Creating and maintaining these family assets is, therefore, key to developing capable students.

▼

Chapter

12

A Family of Contributors

"Who will help me bake the bread?" said the little Red Hen.
"Not I!" said the duck.
"Not I!" said the goose.
"Not I!" said the cat.
"Not I!" said the pig.

—The Little Red Hen, *Byron Barton*

Capable students typically grow up in a home environment in which making contributions is a natural and
expected part of life. While there are many ways to teach
this principle (including volunteerism, service through
religious communities, providing care for extended families), household chores seem to be the most frequently
overlooked—yet the most readily available—opportunity
for most families.

In chapter 5, "Developing Strong Perceptions of Personal Significance," we outlined several principles that help develop a sense of significance in children. This chapter suggests ways to structure everyday, routine events to help meet this need. Chores offer opportunities to teach responsibility, the importance of completing tasks, the distinction between wants and needs, time management, a sense of belonging and significance in the family, and a host of related "real-life" lessons. If one mission of school is preparation for the real world, then family chores can be preparation for schooling, particularly for the work and homework part of schooling.

For many of us, "chores" is a dirty word. It conjures up memories of raking leaves, baling hay, washing windows, cleaning garages, and other unpleasantness. But what is unpleasant to one child is another child's contribution. What chores mean is largely a matter of perception.

Michael and the Farm

Many years ago, when Michael was in college, he had the opportunity to experience how one person can perceive an activity as a chore and another can experience the same activity as an exciting opportunity. A city boy from a metropolis numbering in the millions, Michael went away to college at age seventeen and was teamed up with a roommate from a small dairy town with a population counted in two digits.

When Thanksgiving came and they had a few extra days off, he joined his roommate's family at their home for an introduction to farming life. Guess who was first to wake up at 4:30 each morning, filled with excitement and expectation, ready to milk the cows? For his roommate, this chore was drudgery he had been doing morning after morning and evening after evening all his life; for

Michael, it was new, exciting, and fun. It was a matter of perception.

Marian

Marian was raised in a family in which her mom included her in as many household activities as possible. Her earliest memories center around the many things they did together, both work and play, much of it indistinguishable. One of her earliest memories is of doing the family wash with her mother.

Although she was only two or three years old at the time (and now some thirty years have passed), Marian can still vividly picture the event. Mom's job was to take the wet clothes out of the washing machine and hand them to Marian, who waited expectantly next to her. Marian would then place the pile of wet clothes in the dryer, close the door tightly, press the start button, and stand back, proud of a job well done.

While growing up, Marian was convinced that it took two to do the family wash. For her, helping her mother with the wash was not a chore; it was a contribution.

Marian's mom was very wise. She knew intuitively that her daughter would perceive herself as a significant, contributing member of the family if she gave the little girl opportunities to work *with* her, as an asset. Marian's mom did not treat her child as an object of her orders around the house, or a recipient of her "doing for," as if she were not capable of contributing, but as a real asset in the family, someone without whom the work could simply not be done.

Mom involved her early in life, when she was eager to demonstrate her capability and importance in the family. We often miss those opportunities to involve our children when they are most anxious to be involved, dismissing their efforts because we think they are too young, or because we feel that training them would take too long, or because it just isn't worth the hassle to bother with them.

Thankfully, Marian's mom ignored the temptation to take the easy path and do it all herself; instead, she channeled her little girl's enthusiasm to be involved and to contribute into a cooperative relationship around the house. Today, Marian is a teacher who continues the lessons she learned by providing collaborative learning opportunities and classroom responsibilities for her students so they might see themselves as contributing members of their classroom community.

> **School-Smart Parenting Tip:**
> Involve children in chores as early as possible in life, when they are most willing to participate and more likely to associate work with contributing, rather than with unpleasant tasks forced upon them.

By providing such opportunities at home, we prepare children for the world of school. Students who have experienced contributing at home are more likely to accept responsibilities, do things they might not otherwise care to do, and value their contributions to the school community than are children who lack such opportunities.

Thomas

Not all parents are as wise as Marian's mom. When Michael's son, Thomas, was seven, he approached his dad, who was mowing the lawn. The whole business of mowing a lawn is perceived quite differently through seven-year-old eyes than through thirty-year-old eyes. To Thomas, it looked exciting—the *whirrrr* of the motor, the blades of grass flying out from beneath the machine, the attraction of "men's work," the very ritual of the Saturday morning activity—all thrilled him, and he ran outside, eager to participate.

"Dad, let me help. Watch me. I can do it!" His anticipation was palpable, his interest in participating resolute. His desire to contribute and show Dad that he was a capable young person was undisguised. Thomas was young, innocent, and anxious to be a helper; but Dad shut him out!

"Thomas, I'm very busy," Michael replied. "I don't have time to let you do it now. If you really want to help, go inside and leave me alone."

"But, Dad, I really *do* know how to do it. Come on, just let me do a few rows. I'm not going to hurt the grass. Just let me do a little." Thomas gave it his best shot, so eager to show Dad what he could do, to participate with Dad in the Saturday morning ritual of cutting the lawn, to show his father that he was emerging as a young man himself.

"If you really want to help, Thomas, you'll go inside and play," Michael replied, stubbornly resisting his son's efforts to become a larger part of his life. "Or you'll go watch television. But you really need to leave me alone, son. I'm very busy."

By the time Thomas had reached fourteen, Michael had grown weary of mowing the lawn. He decided it was time to involve Thomas in the activity. This was "men's work," after all, and since Thomas was a young man of fourteen, Michael decided to turn over the lawn maintenance responsibilities to his son.

He approached Thomas with his idea, reminding him that he had many times asked to mow the lawn, and told him that it was now time for him to take over. Thomas's response was unexpected, but understandable.

In his own, inarticulate way, he let Michael know how he felt, which was essentially this: "Dad, seven years ago I went outside and offered to help. I wanted to be part of what you were doing, but you said no. You told me to go inside and play. You told me to go watch television. Well, I've been working at that for the past seven years now, and I've really gotten good at it. I've really got it down now. Sorry."

Luckily for Michael, Thomas decided shortly afterward that he wanted to earn some money through his own efforts, so Thomas began looking for neighbors who needed yard care help. He and his dad made a deal: Michael would give Thomas the initial equipment he would need (mower, edger, extension cords, and such) if he would care for the family yard as well as those of his growing list of customers.

In his mid-twenties now, Thomas has, to date, purchased three new cars and helped finance a college education with the money he earned cutting other people's lawns. Thomas is entrepreneurial by nature, and his work ethic has always been strong. Because of these innate factors, he survived Dad's poor example.

With another child, in other circumstances, the results could have been different. Repeatedly shutting out children—even those with great potential—or failing to involve them in activities, might well produce long-lasting negative perceptions.

Chores can provide an excellent, perhaps essential, training ground for successful schooling, since much of what school requires is work. This is particularly true of school assignments, an important part of which is homework. Examining effective ways to involve children in chores, therefore, is very worthwhile. Following that, we will address the issue of homework, a source of continuing frustration in families with school-age children.

Why Chores?

The business of involving children in household chores is likely to be more successful when planned, organized, and structured than when simply assumed. We have some quite wealthy friends—self-made millionaires in fact. They are pioneers in the grocery store business, and have earned their millions by building successful chains, selling them, then building even more successful chains.

Involving their children in household chores is the last thing they needed to do. Maids, cooks, and grounds-keepers could easily have been hired to spare their children the drudgery of chores. But maids, cooks, and groundskeepers were foreign to their household.

Their children participated, along with them, in all their household chores, and when they were old enough, took outside jobs in local restaurants and grocery stores (just like their middle-class neighbors). Raising their children to know the importance of work and be contributors in the home economy was important to our friends; they planned and organized their family process to teach these values. They would not allow their children to be deprived of the important lessons gained from contributing to their family because of their affluence.

The more we do for and provide for children, the more likely they are to perceive that they are insignificant and what they have to offer is not needed. Indeed, depriving children of the opportunity to do chores by doing everything for them teaches them to be takers, rather than contributors, in life. This undercuts their perceptions of capability and significance that we identified in chapter 4, "Developing Strong Perceptions of Personal Capabilities," and chapter 5, "Developing Strong Perceptions of Personal Significance," as critical to the development of capable students.

When properly organized, chores help children learn the importance of following a task through to its completion. Chores provide opportunities to develop basic work skills such as time management, responsibility, and self-discipline. Being responsible for chores helps children distinguish between wants and needs. It helps them learn that sometimes, for the good of the community (in this case, the family), what we *need* to do is more important than what we *want* to do. This is the foundation of self-discipline (another of The Significant Seven).

Austrian psychologist Alfred Adler called "social interest" the foundation of mental health. Adler, who provided the inspiration for today's positive approaches in family and school discipline, emphasized the importance of seeing oneself as part of a greater community to which we owe involvement, participation, and service. Organizing chores to help children internalize this concept during their earliest years can be vital to their well-being.

And (lest we forget!) chores for children make maintaining the household that much easier for parents. This, however, may well be the least important benefit of chores. They have sufficient value in and of themselves as a vehicle for teaching responsibility, self-discipline, time management, task completion, the perception of significance, and "social interest" . . . even if they added nothing to household cleanliness and neatness!

School-Smart Parenting Tip:
If you want children to develop responsibility,
provide opportunities for them to be
responsible and learn from the experience.

Okay, since chores offer important opportunities for kids, how do we organize a family to take advantage of them? This is one case where the process is more important than the product!

Several years ago, Michael and Carol decided to have an emergency family meeting on chores. Carol, a kindergarten teacher (and therefore one of the hardest working individuals on Earth), felt that she was "getting stuck" with too much responsibility for the household chores. They came together as a family, discussed the issue, and decided that she was right. First they listed the benefits everyone enjoyed because of Mom's income from work. Next, they wrote down all the chores that had to be done each week and discussed what would happen if Mom gave up working in order to stay home and do the chores. No one was happy with that option, so the family considered several other options available (including hiring a domestic with the money Mom made by working outside the home).

They then agreed, through consensus, that the best option was for everyone in the family to take some of the responsibilities. Finally, each family member chose items on the chores list that he or she was willing to do and went to work. (Michael ended up responsible for dinners, so the family soon grew to accept take-out pizza as a staple!)

Organizing the Family for Household Chores

There are a number of ways to successfully organize a family for chores. Tom Sawyer had his unique way. He conned a friend into painting the fence by feigning enthusiasm for the job. The good news is that the trick does work . . . in the short run. After all, Tom's fence did get painted.

But Tom would never again be able to con the same friend that same way. So what we need to look for are long-term ways to involve the family in household chores—ways that, if not effective in involving all members enthusiastically, will at least involve all members out of their sense of responsibility to the family community.

Methods that have been found effective in many families include the following:

- **Provide choices**

As adults we often appreciate being allowed choices in life about what we want to do, how we want to do it, and when we want to do it. Children also appreciate being offered such consideration. (Please note that choices come within limits.)

In a family community, there should be no choice about *whether* or not each family member is going to participate in the household chores. That is a given. *How* each member will participate should be up for discussion.

A very respectful and effective way to do this might be as follows: "Jackie, since we have guests coming over tomorrow, the room you are using needs to be cleaned. Given your plans, when can you have it done?" Notice that there is no debate about *whether* Jackie needs to participate in household chores (and no debate about *who* is responsible for this particular chore, since it is the room she uses), but she is given choices about *when* to do it.

- **Make games of the selection process**

Many families find that making games of the process of selecting chores is an effective way to involve children. A variant of the old truth that "a spoonful of sugar helps the medicine go down," games are probably most effective with very young children. Some families we have worked with in parenting situations have told about spinning wheels they created with the family chores identified in each segment. Each week, each family member spins to find out what their chores for that week will be. The chores would be simple ones that each family member could do, such as sweeping the back patio, cleaning off the table after dinner, dusting the furniture. Adding this little bit of fun and anticipation into the selection process appears to make it that much more acceptable.

- **Do the chores together as a family**

Whenever possible, do the chores together as a family. Raking the backyard leaves is far more enjoyable when done as a family project involving all family members. Establishing a weekly chore time during which all the chores are done by all family members can also help eliminate the drudgery and sense of aloneness that makes chores less than enjoyable.

- **Schedule the chores**

Whether or not you are able to do the chores together as a family, be sure to schedule them. Most people work best with schedules—at home as well as on the job. Provide children with planning calendars to post in their rooms, or, better yet, encourage them to be creative by decorating and designing their own personal planning calendars.

It also helps to have a master schedule somewhere in the common family area. A posted schedule with reminders of which days are garbage days and which are sweep-the-patio days is far more effective than continual nagging. This teaches the importance of scheduling and planning activities and responsibilities, a skill with which many adults still struggle.

- **Create a family chore chart**

Many families have found that a posted family chore chart serves well as a reminder about chores, reducing the nagging that only adds frustration to the whole business of chores. This could vary from a simple listing of family names on a poster or chalkboard along with their chores of the week to a more creative and elaborate system involving pegboards or magnetic displays. Involving children in creating the display further encourages their participation in the chores.

- **Don't "fix" the job the child has done**

Avoid as much as possible the temptation to "fix" the job the child has done. Yes, we can probably clean the room better than the child can; and, yes, if a clean room is our only goal, then we might as well just go ahead and clean it ourselves. However, if our goal is to help a child learn responsibility, contribution, cooperation, and the basic skills of straightening a messy room, we need to involve him or her in the process.

Try to avoid following children around "fixing" their mistakes. Straightening out the covers on beds they have made, or picking up leaves they missed in the backyard, communicates to children that they are not really an asset to the family, that they are not as capable as we would like. Fixing their mistakes sends this message: "I will let you participate in the chores of the house, but, frankly, you're not really capable of doing the kind of job I expect so I'll be right behind you fixing it!"

Using positive words ("Oh, how nice the bed looks!") while you "fix" the job doesn't help! Children may hear the words, but our actions speak so much louder. It may take some effort on our part, but we can learn to live with a less-than-perfectly-made bed. We can say to ourselves, "Okay, the bed isn't made up just the way I would like it to be, but I can be proud that my child made up that bed through his own initiative, and I applaud the effort."

- **Recognize that training takes time**

One reason we often prefer to do tasks ourselves, rather than involve children, is because training takes time. What we often fail to recognize is that the time we spend training them now will pay off in the long run. In the future, we will have less to do ourselves and, more importantly, our children will have been raised to know that responsibilities are an essential part of life.

Taking time for training simply means breaking the chore down into manageable parts, determining what needs to be accomplished in each part, offering some tips (if needed) on how best to accomplish it (allowing for individual differences and choices), and giving specific feedback about results. For example, doing one's wash (something a child can learn very early), can be broken down into separating whites from colors, placing the clothes into the washer, selecting the proper temperature and time setting, pouring in the detergent, closing the lid, and pressing the start button. Each step will require time and practice, and our patience with occasional mistakes, but all will pay off in the long run.

- **Show appreciation by using "I" messages**

There is much debate going on today about the negative effects of praise (as opposed to statements of encouragement, appreciation, or affirmation). To what extent these are more semantic squabbles than real differences of opinion is very much part of that debate.

There should, however, be little doubt that some expressions we can use to show appreciation effectively provide encouragement. Other expressions we use can communicate very different messages. For example, I can tell my daughter that she is a good girl for cleaning her room, or I can tell her that I am pleased with the way she cleaned her room because now I can leave her door open when our guests arrive.

The first approach may suggest to her that her worthiness depends upon what she does and how well she does it. This approach could carry the hidden message that, if she did not clean her room, she might become a "bad girl."

The second approach communicates my feelings about the job she has done. It also lets her know why I might see it as a special contribution. There is no inference that the quality of the job defines her general goodness, badness, or acceptability.

The second example illustrates what are called "I" messages ("I feel _____ about_____ because _____."). Such statements communicate clearly, specifically, and honestly how I feel about what was done and why. By using "I" messages, I accept ownership of my feelings and communicate them honestly. By explaining what I am acknowledging, I give insight. By sharing my reasons for acknowledging the contribution, I help the child to understand my perspective.

If my daughter failed to clean her room, I could say: "Jennifer, I am concerned (my feeling) about the mess in this room (focus on the issue) because our friends are coming by and might want to see our home (explanation of why I am displeased). Since we agreed that it would be cleaned up before they get here, I need to know how soon you can have it done (clear indication of what needs to be done)."

There is no implication that Jennifer's person is being evaluated, no use of adultisms, no blaming or criticizing, just a clear statement pointing out what the problem is and what needs to be addressed. Try using such messages the next time you have an issue . . . you will probably feel better about it, and so will your children.

• **Use family meetings as a vehicle for discussing chores and responsibilities**

Family meetings will be addressed more fully in chapter 14, "Emotional Stability." They can provide a forum for organizing family business, problem solving, and affirming people's contributions. When members of a family sit down together on a regular basis to discuss family needs with a spirit of openness, offer suggestions for problem solving, and try to resolve issues through consensus building rather than through executive edict, children are generally more willing to participate and accept responsibility.

Allowances and Chores

The question of whether or not to give children allowances for chores always reminds us of the Iran-Contra hearings back in the late '80s. Remember Lt. Colonel Oliver North and the Senate investigating committee inquiring into allegations that the United States government had sold arms to Iran in exchange for the release of our hostages, then diverted the money to the Contras in Nicaragua?

It was all very complicated, but those being accused of wrongdoing kept insisting that the deal to sell the arms to their Iranian contacts had nothing to do with the deal to get them to release our hostages. Did you sell arms to the Iranian militants? Yes. Did they then release our hostages? Yes. So you sold them arms so that they would release the hostages? Well, no, not exactly.

What does that have to do with allowances for chores? Frankly, it's a weaselly way of introducing a topic of much debate among those in the business of advising parents on raising their children. Neale S. Godfrey and Carolina Edwards, in *Money Doesn't Grow on Trees* (Fireside), argue that allowances should definitely be given for chores. In the real world, our work is compensated with financial reward, so why not do so for children? They will learn the value of a dollar, the worthiness of work, and the relationship between effort put in and results obtained.

On the other hand, Alfie Kohn, author of *Punished by Rewards: The Trouble with Gold Stars, Incentive Plans, A's, Praise, and Other Bribes* (Houghton Mifflin), cites numerous examples of how pay actually *reduces* the quality of work, since it suggests that the work has no value in and of itself but only in terms of the pay attached to it. Since the work has no intrinsic value, why do anything more than just what is needed to get the promised pay? Kohn further argues against communicating to children that chores, which are part of one's responsibility as a member of the family community, should be compensated with a financial reward.

Our experience on this is much closer to Kohn's: If we want children to see themselves as contributing members of the family, and later as contributing members of their classroom, workplace, and civic communities, then we should divorce the issue of allowances from the issue of household responsibilities. By all means, give children allowances; but, as we discussed previously, try *not* to suggest that allowances are rewards for their accepting responsibilities as contributing members of the family .

Why give them allowances, if not for the chores they do? As members of the family community, children should share in the resources of that community.

One of the most important lessons in life is learning how to manage resources. Allowing children to make financial decisions early in life in safe, supportive settings—and allowing them to experience the consequences of those decisions—gives them practice and training for tougher and more lasting financial decisions. When children are responsible for their own budgets, they can practice the habits of wise spending, saving for future needs, and even giving to charitable causes as part of their responsibility to be of service.

Should you ever compensate children for work done around the house? For their normal daily and weekly chores, we argue no! These are part of their responsibilities to the family.

There are, however, household jobs that we sometimes pay others to do. A good rule of thumb in considering

---

School-Smart Parenting Tip:
Give allowances so your children can
participate in the family resources and
learn to make responsible choices, but
keep allowances separate from chores.

---

whether to pay children for work around the house might
be this: If you would otherwise pay someone outside the
home for a certain job, then offer your children a chance
to contract for doing it. This might include lawn maintenance, "deluxe" style car cleaning, long-term babysitting,
and painting (to name a few of our less-than-exciting
home responsibilities).

If they are interested, ask them to propose a price and
a time frame. If their proposal is acceptable, cut a deal—
but only pay for a completed job, done on time. Do *not*
pay for part of a job (the contractor forfeits the work, if
not done according to the agreement!) and *never* pay by
the hour!

This way children can learn the lessons espoused by
Godfrey and Edwards, on the one hand, and Kohn, on the
other: There are household jobs that we do because we
are members of the family community (intrinsic motivation), and there are jobs beyond normal responsibilities
that we might pay non-family members to do. By giving
children the opportunity to do them, earn extra income,
and learn the "real-world" value of work for pay (external
motivation) in addition to their normal responsibilities,
they learn valuable lessons on both counts.

How early should we start giving allowances? As soon
as children start asking us to buy them things. The first
time a child asks a parent to buy him something is an
excellent teachable moment to talk about allowances. It's

a perfect time to tell our child that toys are given for special occasions, like birthdays; but otherwise, if you want something, you will have to save your allowance and buy it yourself. We will provide you with an allowance because you are a member of the family and should share in the family resources, and we will provide guidance about spending and saving. Now you will have the opportunity to make choices about the things you want.

In short, there are plenty of excellent reasons to give children allowances . . . without the need to tie those allowances directly to chores. Give them allowances, and involve them in household chores, but strive to keep these issues as separate as possible.

Real Contributions

Often we shortchange our children by assuming that they can't do things they are perfectly capable of doing. In our experience working with parents, we have learned numerous ways to involve children in real life chores and activities. In doing so, we communicate to them that they are capable and significant young people who are true assets in the family.

The story of Marian and the washing machine wonderfully demonstrates this, and it provides encouragement for us in our efforts to introduce children to the world of chores and contributions. Michael's failure to involve a seven-year-old son in cutting the grass illustrates what not to do. Examples of providing children with real opportunities to contribute to the family follow:

• In one family, the twelve-year-old son is responsible for clipping grocery coupons from the newspapers and organizing them for use while shopping. In addition to performing a valuable service for his parents, he is learning budgeting, various pricing methods, quantity vs. quality, and the value of saving money (significance, capability, responsibility, and judgment from The Significant Seven). He enjoys the challenge and the opportunity to be with his mom or dad when they do the shopping, often pointing out the better bargains and taking pride in the money he is saving the family.

• In another family, the parents taught their four-year-old to scramble eggs. Mealtimes at their home are often a cooperative experience, with Dad, Mom, and each child contributing to preparing the meal, setting of the table, and cleaning up. The four-year-old has taken a liking to having scrambled eggs instead of cold cereal for breakfast—ever since he was allowed to scramble them for the family.

• One family used the issue of whether or not to get a family pet (in this case a dog), as a way of involving their six-year-old in significant chores. The family would get a dog if Jessie would accept the responsibility of feeding and taking him for walks. She could keep the dog as long as she continued to assume responsibility for him. She made the promise, she followed through, and she learned about responsibility, caring for another, and self-discipline in the process.

• In her family, the fourteen-year-old daughter keeps the family checkbook, making the deposits and paying the bills. In doing so, she is learning about family expenses such as utility costs, mortgage payments, and grocery bills. In addition to the issues of budgeting, saving, deferred gratification, and financial responsibilities, she has learned what "can't afford it" really means in terms of self-discipline and judgment.

Morning Hassles As Opportunities

Of all the irritants that trouble parents today, morning hassles often tops the list. Getting children up and dressed, struggling with breakfast, brushing teeth, and finding backpacks, tennis shoes, and reports that are due first period . . . can lead to stressful mornings and a poor start for the kids in school and for Mom and Dad at work. Getting off to a peaceful, hassle-free, well-organized start in the morning can help, so let's look at the hassles that often result in children starting their school day at less than their best, and identify ways to change negative morning experiences into positive ones.

Viewed from the perspective of household chores, the morning responsibilities that result in hassles are no more difficult to get a handle on than any other responsibilities. In fact, they just need to be treated like any other household responsibilities.

• Use **family meetings** to discuss and clarify responsibilities and concerns related to morning hassles; make sure all family members are allowed to give their input on problems; brainstorm and make a list of all ideas that can help the morning go more smoothly.

• Help children design posters or charts for their room that serve as **reminders** about their morning responsibilities; the more interaction they have with the chart, the better. A chart that necessitates checking off items for which they are responsible on a daily basis is more effective than one that simply lists the items.

• Take time to train children in **organizational skills.** Ask how they might lay out their clothes for the next day and where they can place their book bag and other materials, for example; make sure each child has his own alarm clock and knows how to use it.

- Provide **choices** for morning responsibilities that involve the whole family. For example, having children set the table for breakfast provides opportunities for choices among the various activities . . . such as placing the dishes and silverware; getting the cereal, milk, and juice; cleaning the table when everyone is finished. Use family meetings to provide a forum for the choices.

- Set aside time at the end of each day to talk about the next day and **plan** for what will need to be ready for it.

- Make it a point for all family members to have **responsibilities** in the morning, just as at other times, to reemphasize that chores are a total family affair.

- **Avoid distractions** like TV and video games that not only provide temptations to ignore morning responsibilities, but also disrupt what few moments are available in the morning for family bonding.

Our responsibility as parents is to create the atmosphere and routine that will minimize morning hassles. The more we can involve our children in that task, the better. It's not easy, but the benefit to children and ourselves of a smooth morning, which carries into a smoother day and evening, is well worth the effort.

The benefits to the home of involving and organizing children for chores are a closer, more mutually respectful, more involved, and more committed family whose members see themselves as critical to the success of the family community. The benefits to the child include those attitudes and skills—such as time management, responsibility, and task completion—that are highly valued in the world of work.

Rituals and Traditions

While chores are the most pervasive and most frequently overlooked opportunities for creating a sense of contribution, there are many other ways to meet this need. Probably the easiest and most effective is by establishing family rituals and traditions.

Rituals are defined as "events that involve the same activities and/or sequence of activities." Saying grace before meals, holding hands during grace, blowing out candles on a birthday cake, going around the Thanksgiving table and having each person share what they are thankful for, and decorating family members' graves on Memorial Day are examples of rituals.

Such rituals help children feel they are part of an ongoing process. Rituals encourage bonding and contribute to a child's sense of identity. They are especially valuable when structured to give children a chance to help with their planning and execution.

Traditions are defined as "established practices that occur in various forms over time." Celebrating births and birthdays, attending family reunions, getting together on holidays, and acknowledging significant events (engagements, graduations, rights of passages) are all examples of traditions.

In addition to providing the same opportunities as rituals do, traditions enable children to offer unique ideas, creativity, and talent to the celebrations, as well as present opportunities for children and families to adapt the traditions to their own unique circumstances.

Parents who create and maintain family rituals and traditions provide a sense of constancy and predictability that is sorely lacking in modern society. This offers children a sense of belonging and security that is priceless.

Other Opportunities

Families find many ways to provide a sense of contribution. For example:

- Adopting families at Christmas time
- Doing community service projects together
- Involving children in religious service projects
- Volunteering at nursing homes and health facilities
- Caring for elderly or infirm relatives
- Asking children for advice, help, or counsel
- Providing volunteer child care for community programs
- Becoming a foster family
- Recycling and participating in other environmental projects
- Adopting a child in a foreign poverty area as a family project
- Adopting a highway as a family project
- Planning for and conducting family meetings and events

The most important factor in the above as well as other responsive strategies is that children see themselves as playing an active, contributing role. Specific recognition for service, rather than rewards and generic praise, help reinforce intrinsic motivation and cultivate respect for self and others. These values contribute greatly to a child's success and happiness in school and in life.

Homework

Let's tell it straight, right up front: Homework is between the teacher and the student, not between the teacher and the parent.

Homework is the student's job. It is his or her opportunity to learn self-discipline (defined here as the habit of doing what one *needs* to do rather than what one *wants* to do). It is the child's opportunity to learn responsibility and time management, and to experience the empowering sense of achievement that comes with accomplishing difficult tasks. It is the child's first opportunity to experience accountability to someone other than his parents. To rob our children of these opportunities would be a serious mistake. And yet, in the name of love, we often do exactly that.

A teacher once received the following note from a mom about her seventh-grade child: "We did not have time to study for the history test last night. We looked up the answers and did the vocabulary. Can we take the test tomorrow?"

We did not have time to study for the history test? *We* looked up the answers and did the vocabulary? Can *we* take the test tomorrow? Who is the student here?

Or, as was reported in the January 1996 *Readers' Digest:* "As an English teacher at Marana High School in Tucson, Arizona, I thought I had heard every story about late or missing homework. Then one afternoon a parent walked into my class, handed some papers to her daughter, and said, 'I just finished it. I hope it's not too late for you to turn in.' "

One is tempted to ask whether that parent shows up on test day to take her daughter's exams as well.

Or how about this classic, from Ann Landers' April 4, 1996, column: "I have worked in the same company for over 12 years and have always had a comfortable working relationship with my boss and my colleagues. Yesterday, my boss brought his daughter's fourth-grade homework assignment to me and asked that I or one of my assistants type it up. After much consideration, I walked into his office and told him I thought it was inappropriate for him to ask this. I explained that he was doing a grave disservice to his daughter by not insisting she complete her own homework. I told him I would not do his child's homework, but since he was the boss, I would ask someone else to do it if he so demanded. . . . Today, I found out he personally asked my assistant to complete his daughter's homework . . ."

Hmmm . . . just who is the real boss here?

Resisting the temptation to get too involved in our child's homework is, indeed, difficult. When they come to us with homework questions ("What were the causes of the Civil War?" "How do you pronounce this word?"), we are tempted to give the quick answer to satisfy their immediate need and enable us to get back to our newspaper, TV show, or housework with minimal distraction. But that only serves to communicate two negative messages: (1) We don't have time to give serious attention to our children, and (2) They are incapable of taking the necessary steps to solve their own problems.

Let's consider some alternative approaches. One approach would be to tell our children that their homework is none of our concern, that it's their responsibility, that we paid our homework dues years ago, that we're deeply involved in the newspaper so please don't bother us again. While this may indeed communicate that homework is the child's responsibility, this approach (a good example of hostile permissiveness) communicates also that we are unconcerned about our child's needs. Is the child empowered to do his best in this scenario?

An alternative approach, one that avoids hostile permissiveness and instead communicates genuine concern and empowers the child to have faith in her own abilities, might be demonstrated by the following conversation:

Marcia: Dad, how do you pronounce this word?
Dad: Well, honey, let me take a look here. That's a tough one. I can see why you would have difficulty with it. What tricks have you learned in school to help you sound out a word?

Marcia: We're supposed to break it down part by part and sound out each part and then put them back together, but it isn't working for this one.

Dad: Well, why don't you give it a try. I'll listen carefully and help you if you get stuck. Go ahead.

Let's take a look at this scenario. What perceptions might the child develop from this exchange? That she is a significant enough person that her dad will give her his attention? That she is a capable person who, with a little coaching and guidance, can solve her own problems? That this family environment is a safe one for asking questions, making mistakes, and learning? One would have to answer yes to all three questions.

Note also that Dad does not communicate to Marcia that sounding out the word is easy. By communicating to her that he can understand why she would be having difficulty, he shows respect for her struggle and validates her efforts. In doing so, he creates a safe place for Marcia to share her concerns, which today may only be about homework, but tomorrow may be about boyfriend problems, drugs in school, or career choices. Dad communicates to Marcia, early on, that he is available to hear whatever concerns she has. He will not solve her problems for her, but he will listen empathetically, offer guidance, and affirm her in her struggles.

Or consider this conversation:

Robbie: Mom, what were the causes of the Civil War?

Mom: Well, that sounds like a good homework question. Where do you think you might find the answer?

Robbie: (not in the mood for Mom's parenting class response) I don't know. I left my social studies book in school. Just tell me the answer.

Mom: (unruffled) Well, what other books or resources do we have around the house that might be helpful here?

Robbie: (clearly annoyed now) I don't know. Just give me the answer. It will save time for both of us.

Mom: (not taking the bait) Yes, it would save time for both of us . . . in the short run. But I care for you too much to deprive you of the opportunity to use your own abilities to solve this problem, so let me try again. Where else might you find the answer to your question besides your social studies book?

Robbie: (really irritated now) Things were lots easier around here before you started going to those stupid parenting classes! Forget it. I'll just go ask Dad. Dad, what were the causes of the Civil War?

Dad: (wisely taking the cue from Mom) Well, that sounds like a good homework question. Where do you think you might find the answer?

Robbie: (angrily stomping off toward the bookshelf holding the encyclopedias) Forget it! I'll just look it up in the encyclopedia.

Mom and Dad: (together, in more ways than one) Great idea. Let us know how it works out.

What is Mom (and Dad, who also took the parenting course) doing here? She refuses to rescue her child and, instead, continues to put the ball back in his court. She respectfully validates his efforts, but she also declines to take responsibility away from him. She communicates confidence in his ability to solve his own problems. And she does not allow Robbie's anger to become a separate, distracting issue.

The first step in solving homework hassles is recognizing that homework is the student's, not the parents' responsibility. When we consistently follow through on that basis, supporting our children's efforts and offering guidance where appropriate in the process, we effectively lay the foundation for a more pleasant experience with homework. But this issue of homework involves much more than just recognizing it as the child's responsibility.

Let's look at specific concerns that continually surface regarding this important aspect of schooling.

School-Smart Parenting Tip:
Homework is the child's, not the parents' responsibility. By enforcing that early—with encouragement, empathy, and support—we lay the foundation for our children developing as capable young people who understand the meaning of personal responsibility.

"Homework Is So Boring!"

Michael once had a history professor who would say that to the interesting person, everything is interesting; to the boring person, everything is boring. Michael's own children never reacted favorably to his quoting that, so it's probably not an effective approach.

Yes, it would be wonderful if homework were always exciting, chores were always thrilling, all jobs in the "real world" stimulating, and all our varied responsibilities as parents, spouses, employees, and employers were enjoyable. But since that will never be the case, it's probably more effective to accept this fact: Yes, homework may well be boring at times. Then move on from there, confident that there are also some excellent reasons for homework, boring though it may be.

Why homework? In the early school years, homework is given largely to provide opportunities for children to learn responsibility and study habits. Reinforcement of knowledge and specific skills is secondary to the more important goal of developing the basic habits that serve children so well in later years.

In the middle grades, reinforcing knowledge and skills is the primary value of homework, while developing responsibility and study habits runs a close second. Not until the later years, during college and graduate school, do personal enrichment and discovery become the primary values of homework. But if a child does not develop the habits of taking responsibility and studying in the early years, his opportunity for personal enrichment may never occur.

When to Do Homework

Let's face it: We adults are not all alike in terms of energy level. Why should we expect our children to be? Some of us are morning people; others don't get started until 10 or 11 A.M.

Michael is a morning person. Typically, he's up at 4:45 A.M., out the door for a morning jog by 5:45 A.M., and at work by 7:30 A.M. His friend Tom, on the other hand, swears he's never seen 4:45 A.M. and even doubts there is such a thing. He struggles out of bed at 8 A.M., is at work by 9 A.M., . . . and wakes up sometime around 10:30 A.M. By 3 P.M., when Michael is placing toothpicks in his eyes to keep them open, Tom is enjoying his daily exercise routine. By 10 P.M.,Tom's ready to hit the town, and Michael is setting his alarm for the next morning. All of us have different internal clocks, and we need to respect the differences in our children, just as we respect them in adults. When is the best time to do homework? For some, right after school is ideal. For others, just before or just after dinner is best. Some prefer late at night just before retiring, and still others find in the morning before going to school works well. We parents need to respect and allow for differences. How can we demonstrate that respect? The following dialogue, which might take place during a beginning-of-the-year family meeting, might prove effective:

> Dad: Here's an interesting agenda item—homework. Rebecca, what are your plans for doing your homework this year?
>
> Rebecca: Well, last year I did it right after school because I found that I got too distracted with telephone calls later in the evening, but I don't think that will work this year because of track practice. I think I'll try to get on a right-after-dinner schedule.
>
> Dad: What problems might that cause you with telephone calls and other distractions?
>
> Rebecca: I'm going to tell my friends not to call me until after 8 o'clock . . . and use my message recorder for those who forget!
>
> Dad: Sounds like a great idea. Let me know how it works.

What if our children have difficulty making an effective choice? How can we guide them while respecting their need to make choices? Let's look at the following dialogue:

> Dad: Andy, what are your plans for doing your homework this year?
>
> Andy: Oh, I'll probably do it just before going to bed. That's when I did it last year.
>
> Dad: Well, how did that work out last year? I recall some communication from the school regarding missed homework.

Andy: Yeah, but that was just during soccer season when we had those late night games . . . and during basketball season when the coach had those late meetings . . . and during. . . . Well, maybe right after school would be a better idea.

Dad: How do you feel right after school? Do you need a break of any kind?

Andy: I like to get a quick snack. After that I think I can get right to my homework.

Dad: Great idea. And I'd like to pass on something that I heard just the other day about this stuff. If you break up your homework and studying into smaller chunks, taking occasional breaks here and there, it will work out better. Apparently, we're more alert at the beginning and the end of our work, so if we can create more beginnings and ends by breaking up the work into several pieces, we retain what we are learning better. You might want to give that a try. Let me know how it works out.

Notice that Dad is able to offer his own guidance based on past experience, plus a helpful bit of information he recently picked up—in a respectful manner that allows his son individual choices. Notice too that he recognizes the plan as his son's and demonstrates an interest in how it would turn out. Offered with sincerity, such comments communicate that the child deserves to be treated with dignity as he works through life's little challenges—a powerful lesson to communicate.

Where to Do Homework

The same principle that addresses the question of when to do homework should govern the question of where and under what circumstances to do homework. How many of us have spent small fortunes on fancy desks and chairs for our children, only to discover that they prefer to read in bed? Some children prefer to work in their rooms; others feel too isolated there, and learn much more effectively at the kitchen table. Some people work best in an environment of total quiet; others find quiet unnerving and need background music. In fact, some studies indicate that classical music is particularly helpful in studying, and certain evidence even suggests that children labeled attention deficit and hyperactive can focus better with rock music playing in the background. (Come to think about it, John, Paul, George, and Ringo were quite instrumental—pardon the pun—in getting many of the "Beatles" generation through high school math homework.)

The bottom line is this: What matters is that the homework is done, according to the style of the child. Learning styles vary immensely, and it is good to remember that what one person sees as distraction, another person sees as familiar and comfortable.

"What if My Child Refuses to Do Homework?"

Frankly, whether to do homework is not an option. *When* to do the homework, *how* to do the homework, and *where* to do the homework—those are options; but *whether* or not to do the homework should not be an option.

If we raised our children with household chores, affirmed them as capable young people, empathetically supported their efforts and struggles, communicated interest without getting overly involved in their homework (all within an emotionally stable environment), then the odds are remote that they will seriously ignore their homework or other responsibilities. But if they do experience difficulty fulfilling homework responsibilities, then go through a mental checklist to determine a possible cause.

If they have not had experience with household chores, then it's time to discuss the topic at a family meeting. If we made an issue of grades, perhaps even conveyed that our love for them is somehow tied to the grades our children receive, we need to let go of that and communicate our unconditional love. If we have not shown interest in their schooling or homework, they may perceive it as unimportant; it's time we make the effort to get into their quality world and find out what's going on in their lives. And if we have become *too* involved, perhaps even doing our children's homework for them, we need to back off, to wean them from depending on us (or wean ourselves from needing their dependence on us), and reaffirm them as capable people who can accomplish things on their own.

In working with our children on the homework issue, it is important that we not panic and regress to either an overly strict or an overly permissive approach. The overly strict approach looks for the quick fixes that result from the authoritarian now-you're-going-to-do-it-my-way attitude. The permissive approach basically says, "I give up. It's not worth the hassle. Do whatever you want. It's your life." The strict approach results, at best, in short-term improvements with no internal change in the child. The permissive approach communicates the message that we no longer care. Neither is effective—nor respectful.

Instead, continue to seek the root causes of the problem, identified above, and be willing to accept the fact that things may get a bit worse before they get better. Be patient, give choices regarding the incidentals, be firm in communicating the non-negotiables, and be respectful at all times.

But what if my child won't do his homework by himself, but continually asks me how to do this and how to do that? Again, look for root causes. Might your child simply want your attention? If so, firmly and respectfully tell him it is important that he do his work himself, but as soon as he is finished, the two of you will read a story, play a game, go for a walk, or do whatever your favorite activity is, together. This communicates that you do want to spend time with him and are willing to give him attention when appropriate, but that he also has responsibilities he must do on his own.

There are no shortcuts to taking responsibility for homework. Yes, you can punish your children by grounding them and taking away their diversions, but that will only have short-term effects. Such external measures will not develop the self-reliance and responsibility the child needs. For self-reliance and responsibility, we need to provide the long-term approach of effective parenting, not defective punishing. It takes time and commitment . . . and the decision on our part to change our own lives so our children will be inspired to change theirs. We cannot change others; we can only change ourselves.

Homework, Grades, and Rewards

All that we previously said about rewards for chores (allowances) applies equally to rewards for completed homework or good grades. In short, avoid such rewards at all costs.

Giving rewards for homework or grades communicates to the child that the homework or test or project has no intrinsic value. By providing external rewards, we contribute to the perception that schooling is irrelevant to the real world, except to the part that connects rewards to work. A major philosophical question in education deals with the very purpose of schooling. Is the goal of education best explained in terms of the classical values of seeking truth, goodness, and beauty? Is its purpose more cultural—for example, promoting the values of the Amer-

> **School-Smart Parenting Tip:**
> Avoid giving your child rewards for
> good grades or completed assignments;
> instead, help him see his accomplishments
> as valuable in themselves, not as means
> toward the attainment of rewards.

ican people? Is it more ethical—promoting what is right and proscribing what is wrong? Is it more utilitarian—teaching the skills necessary to get a job? Is it parental survival—giving us some time each day away from the kids?

No doubt, American education is all these things. But raising our children to expect rewards for fulfilling their responsibilities at school narrows the focus considerably; it models only those aspects of schooling that promote assimilation into the world of work for compensation. If we want our children to experience more from their schooling than the perception that its sole value is to ready them for the world of work, then we would do well to avoid the temptation to reward them for completing their assignments and for getting good grades.

Does this mean we should avoid all forms of recognition and celebration for our children's school achievements? Not at all. It means only that we should avoid communicating to them that rewards are the expected outcome for all accomplishments.

Over the years, we have worked with many families who have taken that concept to heart, switching from taking their children out to dinner as a reward for a good report card to taking them out to dinner to celebrate the successful close of the semester, regardless of the grades received. The celebration is the same: The family goes out to eat. But in the earlier version, the children perceived their parents' attention had to be earned by good grades. Now they view the dinner as a family event celebrating their efforts, regardless of specific achievement. Earned attention or family celebration—such a small change—can make such a huge difference.

The Do's and Don'ts of Parental Involvement in Homework

Finally, let's sum up our discussion of homework by reviewing some do's and don'ts about parental involvement:

Do's	Don'ts
Do show interest in children's homework by listening when they talk about it or ask for help.	**Don't** get overly involved by doing children's homework for them
Do communicate empathy for their struggles.	**Don't** communicate that the homework is easy and that the child should have learned it three grades ago.
Do communicate that even though the work may be difficult, you still have confidence that children can do it.	**Don't** communicate that the work is too hard and that the teacher should know that children shouldn't be expected to do such hard work.
Do allow choices in when, where, and under what conditions children will do homework.	**Don't** demand that the homework be done at this specific time, in this specific place, under these specific conditions.

Do offer guidance if they get stuck; for example, share tricks you have learned for completing homework quicker, or resources you have found that might provide answers or help.

Do recognize effort with sincere and specific words of encouragement: "I really like what you did on that science project because you worked on it all by yourself, you learned a lot about nutrition as a result, and you got to teach me some things I didn't know as well."

Do take the opportunity of homework to provide that safe place for children to seek you out and receive comfort and support.

Don't communicate that you don't have time to listen to problems or concerns because, after all, you have problems of your own.

Don't use meaningless words of praise: "Great science project!" (Why is it great? What did the child learn from it?) Also, avoid rewards for homework or grades, as these communicate that the work has little value in itself.

Don't miss the opportunity to have one-on-one time with your children just because you are too busy with TV, the newspaper, housework, etc.

Will all this necessarily result in a long-lasting love affair between your child and her homework? Of course not. It will, however, provide a supportive and encouraging setting in which she can test her own abilities, make her own choices, follow through on her own plans, and take responsibility for an important part of her schooling. The lessons she learns will carry over into the "real world" of jobs, families, and communities. So take ownership of this first behavior in raising children for success and happiness in school: Start today by organizing your family to share responsibility for household chores. Then when it comes time for homework, you can help your children successfully transfer the habit of taking responsibility to their schoolwork and enable them to experience pride in their own accomplishments.

▼

Chapter

13

An Affirming Family

There were two things about Mama. One is she always expected the best of me. And the other is that then no matter what I did, whatever I came home with, she acted like it was the moon I had just hung up in the sky and plugged in all the stars. Like I was that good.

—Barbara Kingsolver, *The Bean Trees*

Another asset of highly effective families is the ability to convey affirmation by celebrating and cultivating the unique talents, abilities, and personality of each member. We define affirmation as "evidence or confirmation of a person's worth, significance, value, acceptability, contributions, etc."

When we get involved and show real interest in a child's interests, we communicate a sense of respect for the child as a person. We confirm that the child has the right to individuate from us, and even though we might have much to share from our wisdom and experiences, the child too has much to share with us out of his or her uniqueness. In short, we affirm the child as a significant person whose interests are valid and whose individuality is respected . . . a person in his or her own right.

Involvement is currently a hot topic in parent/school communication. Educational leaders uniformly stress the importance of parents' getting involved in their children's schools, and most literature on parenting recommends the same. Parents are frequently urged to attend school functions, join the PTA, show up for parent conferences, and get to know the teachers. And teachers routinely list lack of parental involvement among their major concerns. All of this is, of course, very much on target.

However, it is possible to be involved without being sincerely interested. It is also possible to be sincerely interested but not involved. We suspect that the emphasis is placed on the wrong word. Is it the *involvement* that is so important? Or is it also important that parents communicate to children a sincere *interest* in what they are doing?

These two words are not mutually exclusive. We can be both involved and interested. But our fear is that in emphasizing involvement, we may forget the real reason for getting involved in the first place, namely sincere interest in our children. Let's take a closer look at this.

Interest and Involvement

How important, first, is involvement? In August 1995, the Family Involvement Partnership for Learning, a coalition of some 140 educational organizations throughout the country, published a challenge to American families and communities to get involved in their schools.

In an introduction to their publication, they wrote: "When families, educators, and communities work together, schools get better and children get the quality education they need to lead happy, productive lives." The coalition went on to argue that the more parents get involved in their children's schools, the more they will learn what's going on in them, the more they will discover ways to contribute time and talent to them, and the more they will be attuned to potential concerns. No argument there.

"Schools are the responsibility of all of us." "There is no commitment without involvement." "It takes a whole village to raise a child." All are familiar clichés; but the reason they are clichés is because they are true. No argument.

But it is possible for parents to become over-involved! Parents can become so fearful of letting go, so desirous of advancing their own agenda for their children's lives, that they cannot stay away from the school!

Educators frequently encourage parents to check their children's homework. However, anecdotal evidence suggests that many parents get so involved in their children's homework that one might ask: "Is it really the child's work?" Children, faced with such parental behavior, may be shortchanged in their opportunities to benefit from their own education because of too much parental involvement.

In fact, a good argument could be made that many parents become overly involved in almost every aspect of their children's lives. They are a central part of their children's school activities, their social activities, and even their play. The very concept of "free play" becomes all but lost.

Some parents feel guilty when they are not entertaining children, or shuttling them from a friend's house to the park to the movies to the mall. They organize their sons' and daughters' sports activities, parties, and games, thereby depriving children of the opportunity to learn organizational skills for themselves.

They sign their children up for this activity and that activity, filling every moment of their lives with things to do, things largely of a parent's choosing. Later they wonder why, during those few times they have neglected to plan activities for them, the children complain of being bored. Never having had the opportunity to organize their own activities, such children have become dependent on parents to plan and provide for them, and when that doesn't happen, they are lost . . . and bored.

Given the potential for over-involvement, we prefer to avoid the term. Rather than recommend that parents get *involved* in schools, we recommend they take an *active interest* in what children are learning and doing. Please note that interest does not preclude or supplant involvement; it simply shifts the focus.

The benefits are the same. Parents still learn what's going on in the schools, how they can contribute to young people's success, what's happening politically that might affect their children, and so on. But focusing on interest rather than involvement means fewer liabilities.

By becoming actively interested in children's lives, parents tend to learn about their children's unique strengths and talents, their hobbies, their perceptions, their needs, and the special ways they can contribute to the family and school. They are better able to avoid the temptation of getting too involved and over-controlling children's lives.

"I Didn't Turn Out to be the Baseball Player My Father Wanted Me to be."

On a radio talk show some time ago, the subject for the evening was how to write an autobiography. The host put this question to the listening audience to generate call-in responses: "What would be the first line of your autobiography?" The very first caller responded: "I didn't turn out to be the baseball player my father wanted me to be."

What a powerful indictment! The first line of this person's autobiography, the statement that sums up the most significant aspect of his life, is that he didn't fulfill the agenda his father had prescribed for him. His life is summarized in terms of a great disappointment, one resulting from his father's placing his personal interest over his child's interests. Sadly, many of us make the same mistake. Michael's story, which follows, is all too common.

A Liberal Arts Nerd, Just Like Me

By the time our adopted son, Thomas, had come to us at the age of six months, we already had his life planned out for him. He would attend the finest private elementary and secondary schools we could afford, go on to the same liberal arts university that both his mother and I had attended, study literature and philosophy and history and the arts, and join our ranks as a fellow teacher on our mission to transform the world through education.

It sure made sense to me: Who wouldn't want to be a liberal arts nerd, just like me? What else in life is worth striving for?

Well, Thomas would have none of it. He resisted our efforts to remake him in our own image. Instead, he charted out a course (subconsciously at first, then quite deliberately as he matured) that would lead him in an entirely different direction. And we, wanting to be good parents, resisted him, insisting that we knew best. But Thomas's will was stronger, and his course prevailed. And we are truly thankful for it.

The mistake we made was common. We *assumed* (remember the barriers?) that Thomas's interests and talents would be the same as ours. Or worse, we assumed that we could fashion interests and talents for him rather than affirm him for who he was.

Thomas is unique, as are all of us, and his interests and talents would emerge from within himself, not from our outside pressure. Thomas would have none of the liberal arts.

An extremely hard worker who will read extensively to prepare for a test, he has never "read for pleasure" in his life, and probably never will. His orientation is as far from the liberal arts as one can get; his talents are, instead, entrepreneurial. He can evaluate business opportunities, know instinctively when (and when not) to make major purchases, choose the best investment strategies, and work extreme hours to accomplish results.

He would struggle interminably over a textbook math problem that involves calculating interest on a bank account, but he can determine intuitively the effect of various interest rates on his *own* accounts. Such is the nature of his talent.

Thomas began to blossom when we began to back off. When we dropped our agenda for him, he discovered his own and took flight. When we decided to stop involving ourselves in his education and started instead to take an active interest in him, the pressure was released and he had a chance to realize his potential.

Demonstrating Genuine Interest in Children's Interests

Dropping our own agenda for our son was difficult for us, but once we dropped it, an undeniable burden was released as well, a burden for both us and him. In looking back and trying to identify what allowed us to drop our agenda, we identified three contributing behaviors. First was Thomas's tenacity; he knew what he wanted and he went for it, in spite of our failure to comprehend.

The second behavior was our own conscious effort to listen more carefully to what was on his mind; listen to what he was saying when he returned from work or school or a movie with friends; listen to what he was saying when he was not prompted by our questions; and listen to what came forth from *his* agenda. If you want to find out what your child's real interests are, observe him when no one is telling him what to do and when you are not actively involved with him.

The third behavior was making a concerted attempt to understand Thomas. Our previous attempts to get into Thomas's world (once we grudgingly accepted that he had a separate world) were clumsy. We struggled awkwardly, as many parents do, and our attempts at meaningful dialogue followed a pattern that is all too familiar:

Dad: How was school today, Son?
Thomas: Fine.
Dad: So what happened in school today?
Thomas: Nothin'.
Dad: Well, did you have a good day?
Thomas: Yeah.

Change occurred when we decided to wait for Thomas to comment on his day without our prompting, listen carefully to his comment, and then engage him in conversation about it. The more he felt that we were sincerely interested in what was going on in his world, the more he would open up . . . and the more interested we actually became in the things that interested him. If communication with your child is a problem, remember this: If he does not respond to your questions, stop asking questions and listen to what he *does* say, then build the conversation around that.

Don't Just Hear—Listen!

Ever since Thomas was old enough to pick up a ball, we would spend time together (daily when he was a toddler, maybe weekly during his elementary school years) throwing the ball around. That was the expression we used: "throwing the ball around." In spring and summer, it was a baseball; in fall and winter, a football. In either case, we were "throwing the ball around."

What I never realized during all those years was that for Thomas, "throwing the ball around" was a form of communication with his dad. "Throwing the ball around" had little to do with the mechanics of sport for him; it was all about being with his dad, one-on-one, and communicating.

It hit home finally when he was in his mid-teens and came to me one Saturday and said, "Hey, Dad, let's go out and throw the ball around." My reply indicated that I had no sense whatsoever of what he was asking me.

I had no sense that Thomas was saying, in his own way: "Dad, you've been ignoring me for some time now, and I'd like a little of your time to chat. But I really don't know what to chat about, and if I start talking to you now while you're reading the paper, you probably won't listen anyway. So let's go outside and throw the ball around because when we do that you have to pay attention to me—if for no other reason than to avoid getting beaned on the head!"

But hearing only the words "let's throw the ball around" coming from a fifteen-year-old with plenty of friends, I replied: "Thomas, you don't need me to throw the ball around anymore. You're fifteen years old. Go throw the ball around with your friend David." Thomas just walked away.

My reply to Thomas was literally correct; he didn't need me to throw the ball around anymore. But that was not what he really wanted. He wanted to be with his dad. And, although I heard his words, I wasn't *listening* to him. I never stopped to ask myself, "What could Thomas really be asking me? He has friends to throw the ball around with. Why is he asking me to be with him?" If I had asked—if I had listened, not just heard—I would not have shut him out of my life.

When we hear, we pick up the content. When we listen, we pick up both the content and the context. The content—throwing the ball around—was easy to grasp. The context—a fifteen-year-old who wanted some time with his dad—required a deeper level of attention. It required listening.

Practice listening. Look for the context, not just the content. Tune in to what your children are really saying. Show real interest in them.

Interest Requires Respect

When we show real interest in what is going on in another person's world, we affirm that person by offering our deepest respect. When we substitute our world for that of the other, we show a lack of respect.

Neil

Neil Perry, the central character in the motion picture *Dead Poets' Society,* discovered an interest in the world of the theater. He tried out for and won the lead role in *A Midsummer's Night's Dream* and received the admiration of his fellow students and teachers for his performance.

In astonishment, he found himself saying at the end of the performance, "I was good. I was really good." He had found something, the theater, that he truly loved, excelled at, and was determined to pursue.

However, his father would have none of it. He had sent his son to Welton Academy to receive the educational foundation he would need to go on to Harvard and then become a doctor (Dad's agenda), not to dissipate his energies in the theater (Neil's agenda). When his efforts to prevent his son's involvement in the school drama program failed, Mr. Perry decided to take more forceful action and withdraw Neil from the school. Deprived of the one thing he really wanted, what gave him true pleasure, what provided him an outlet for his new-found talent, Neil ended it all in the tragic climax of the movie.

This is, of course, an extreme reaction to parental control over a young person's life. But it demonstrates clearly, if a bit dramatically, the disrespect we show when we substitute our own agenda for our children's agendas.

Billy

Billy, twelve years old and in the seventh grade, is the first-born of a family of four. Studies in birth order suggest that firstborn children tend to demonstrate perfectionism. They tend to be over-achievers, and are often overly critical of themselves and others.

Since their only older role models are parents—unlike any brothers or sisters who follow them, who will have brothers or sisters for older role models—firstborns often develop the perception that they must be perfect, as they perceive their parents to be. To reach that perfection, they tend to push the envelope of their capabilities, become overly critical of their mistakes, and demonstrate impatience with the shortcomings of others.

These perceptions tend to surface in firstborns even with no push in that direction from their parents. Unfortunately, Billy's parents actively reinforced those perceptions, communicating clearly that his job was to justify them to their neighbors. In other words, Billy was to be perfect, as they were perfect, in all things. "See our perfect son! See how he reflects on our own perfection? See what model parents we are!" Such was Billy's world, as he perceived it and as his parents actively shaped it.

The problems started early. In fact, they started the first day of kindergarten. Billy's parents had dressed him to perfection, combed and greased down every last hair, and instructed him, for the umpteenth time, on what they expected of his academic and behavioral performance. He was reminded to sit up straight, to use the right utensil when eating lunch, to avoid slurping his milk, to flush after using the commode, to print his name clearly, to keep his shirt tucked in, to check the shine on his shoes after playing outside, and on and on and on.

When Billy approached the classroom door, five years of anxiety erupted within him. He threw himself to the floor and kicked and screamed with wild abandon. He cried and pleaded and tore at his clothes. He begged his parents to take him home. He simply could not handle that environment. The expectations were just too much. Such was Billy's introduction to school.

Billy struggled throughout his elementary school years. His social skills were extremely poor, in spite of the fact (or, perhaps, because of the fact) that he grew up in an extremely social-conscious and proper family. He had terrible difficulty getting along with his classmates, appearing to enjoy zeroing in on their weak points and terrorizing them verbally.

He was particularly insensitive to weakness or imperfection. The only teachers he would mind were the more authoritarian ones. Any teacher who tried to model a more respectful style would be fair game. Billy perceived respectfulness and gentleness as indicators of weakness, and he hated weakness.

As you might guess, Billy spent his elementary school years in near-continuous trouble. He alienated his classmates, he alienated his teachers, and even appeared to alienate his parents, who would often shift discussion from Billy to their other children, who were not experiencing such difficulties.

His parents had trouble accepting that Billy's difficulties stemmed from the pressure they had placed on him early in life, and which they continued to place on him. Desirous of having the perfect family, they feared relaxing their grip on Billy, lest he rebel totally. Finally, we convinced them that he had *already* rebelled, and that they would need to back off if they expected him to return.

Billy is seventeen now. After four years of family counseling, his parents and teachers are noticing slow but steady progress. His social skills are improving. He is beginning to accept the fact of his own imperfection, and the imperfection of others. But how much was lost in the process?!

Billy's parents raised him to be perfect. Through counseling, it became apparent that Dad demanded perfection of his wife, and she in turn assumed that her responsibility was to demand it of the children. The father was a highly motivated achiever, who expected the same of those working under him—at the office and at the home.

Like Neil Perry's dad, Billy's parents had a chiseled-in-granite plan for Billy. But whereas the plan for Neil was quite specific—he was to go on to Harvard and become a doctor—the plan for Billy was more general, though nonetheless demanding—he was only worthy of affirmation when he managed to be perfect, in all things.

Billy's parents were not interested in their son's interests or in his world. They were interested, instead, in his fitting a pattern, a mold they created in their own minds. He couldn't do it, so he rebelled.

Perhaps somewhere along the line, Billy would have benefited from hearing the story of Babe Ruth, whose 714 homeruns were scattered among almost twice as many strikeouts. Babe's success/failure ratio was outdone by slugger Hank Aaron, the man who made baseball history by topping the Babe in both the homerun and strikeout categories: 755 and 1,383 respectively. Yet no one would call either man a failure!

> **School-Smart Parenting Tip:**
> Teach children that mistakes are essential
> to learning. Don't ask, "Why did you
> make that mistake?" Ask instead
> "What did you learn from that mistake?"

Since affirmation includes demonstrating respect for the uniqueness of each child, it is helpful to look at some of the many ways that children demonstrate their uniqueness. Personalities and behavior styles, interests, talents, intelligence styles, and even birth order are some of the more dramatic ways through which children express their individuality.

Personality and Behavior Styles

About 2,500 years ago, a Greek philosopher by the name of Hippocrates hypothesized that there were four basic personality styles. He further hypothesized that, although each person is a mixture of these basic personality styles, each also tends to possess a dominant style that affects how he or she behaves more often than not. Hippocrates' four styles have come down to us through the ages as the choleric (dominant, forceful, "testy"), sanguine (cheery, outgoing, extroverted), phlegmatic (composed, impassive, easygoing), and melancholic (introspective, cautious, moody) styles.

Since Hippocrates' time, there have been numerous attempts to identify personality and behavior styles. The result of this process is a fascinating look at individual strengths and weaknesses, goal orientations, motivations, and unique ways to serve the organization, family, or community.

Some argue that systematic approaches to understanding people contain an internal danger, that of reducing people to stereotypes and communicating a deterministic model that denies the uniquely human potential to change and grow. Critics of such approaches remind us that, through creativity and imagination, people are capable of transcending their present conditions, rewriting their present script, and learning new behaviors and discarding old ones. We believe this is true. When using any scheme of describing, it is healthy to steer clear of the temptation to stereotype. For whatever reasons, individuals demonstrate some typical styles in responding to everyday situations. For example, by nature, an individual may be introverted and introspective and enjoy being alone. While this might accurately describe one's preferred style, it does not determine how this individual will always respond. If the situation calls for it, the individual can be outgoing and sociable, though such responses may not come naturally. However, he or she might still prefer to be home alone with a good book.

One way to show genuine interest in children is to make the effort to understand their unique personality styles—and we don't need a personality style assessment instrument to do this. We just need to listen to and observe them to enter and try to understand their worlds.

Does a child need a great deal of alone time, or does he or she need the continual presence of others? Does the child tend to be task-oriented, or more people-oriented? Process thoughts slowly or quickly? Inwardly or externally? Through reflection or through discussion? Awareness of these questions is the first step to understanding a child's unique behavior style, and the journey from awareness to respect can be short one, if we work at it.

The way we interact with others is very much a function of our unique behavior style. Some children make friends easily. For others, the word "friends" will be used very restrictively. Some children will be "take-charge" types, leading their classmates in adventure after adventure; others prefer to follow. Some will be task-oriented, focusing on the job at hand and paying less attention to the other people involved; others will be more people-oriented, placing the task at hand in a secondary position to the immediate needs of the people involved.

Remember that the Golden Rule doesn't always work in interpersonal relationships. Treating others according to their preferences, rather than our own, is more effective. Do unto others not as you would have done unto you, but as they would have done unto themselves.

In efforts to get into a child's world, be careful not to assume that he or she wants to be treated as we do. The child may need to be left alone when feeling down, whereas we may prefer to be with others. Respect that need.

Your child may prefer just a few good friends, even though you may be friends with everyone in the community. Again, respect that preference. Your child may prefer private recognition, even though you prefer public recognition. One more time: Affirm the child by respecting that preference.

Multiple Intelligences and Talents

One of the healthiest discoveries of recent times is the understanding that intelligence is much more than that which is measured by standard IQ tests. Two recent books, Daniel Goleman's *Emotional Intelligence* (Bantam Books) and David Lazear's *Seven Ways of Knowing* (Skylight), have been particularly instrumental in broadening our understanding of intelligence and opening us up to a greater appreciation and respect for the diversity of human intelligence.

Our ability to affirm children is strengthened when we open ourselves to the possibility that their intelligence is expressed in different ways from our own. We allow ourselves to see things in them that we would not otherwise be able to see.

The more we know about the diversity of intelligences in the world, the better equipped we are to help children tap into their particular strengths, shore up any relative weaknesses, and become more well-rounded individuals. These are important resources as they progress through the school years.

The pioneering work in the area of recognizing and identifying multiple intelligences was done during the early 1980s by Harvard researcher Howard Gardner. Gardner's work is most recently popularized by David Lazear who, in *Seven Ways of Knowing,* explores the seven specific intelligences previously identified by his mentor, Gardner. Careful not to close the book on additional intelligences not yet recognized as such, both Gardner and Lazear point out that the identification of seven intelligences is somewhat arbitrary.

In fact, at one point Gardner identified as many as twenty distinct intelligences. But the seven classifications of intelligences at which they arrived effectively communicate the thesis that intelligence is not one-dimensional but is, instead, broad and diverse.

In the following thumbnail descriptions, see if you can identify the particular strengths of your children:

- **Verbal/Linguistic**—the ability to use words and language effectively and creatively in writing, reading, speaking, and listening; the child with strong verbal/linguistic intelligence will excel in activities that require good communications skills, critical thinking, and exchanging ideas.

- **Logical/Mathematical**—the ability to think abstractly, to recognize patterns, and to see connections between separate pieces of information; the child with strong logical/mathematical intelligence will excel in activities that require conceptual organization such as strategic planning, program design, and product development.
- **Visual/Spatial**—the ability to form images and pictures in the mind and to work effectively with patterns, shapes, physical relationships, and colors; the child with strong visual/spatial intelligence will excel in activities that require a talent for aesthetic design, architecture, and the creative arts.
- **Body/Kinesthetic**—the ability to use the body to express emotion (as in dance), to play a game (as in athletics), or to create (as in making a new invention); the child with strong body/kinesthetic intelligence will excel in activities that require physical dexterity such as sports, dance, and mechanics.
- **Musical/Rhythmic**—the ability to recognize and direct rhythmic and tonal patterns in creative ways; the child with strong musical/rhythmic intelligence has the ability to stir the emotions through musical sound (and he's probably tapping his pencil on the table as he's doing his homework!).
- **Interpersonal**—the ability to deal effectively with others in relationships and communication; the child with strong interpersonal skills will excel in activities that require working with others, being sensitive to others, and leading others; this may well be the most "useful" intelligence.
- **Intrapersonal**—the ability to reflect upon the self and understand one's own feelings and emotions;

the child with strong intrapersonal intelligence will excel in activities that require thoughtful reflection.

The challenge for parents reflecting on these seven intelligences is not so much to identify children's particular strengths (although that is important in fulfilling our commitment to respect their uniqueness), but to raise consciousness about the diversity of intelligence. Through this increased consciousness, parents may effectively create a home environment that maximizes the potential for children to experience and realize that diversity.

If these seven intelligences represent the fullness of individual capability, then it would be worthwhile to seek ways to expose that fullness to children. Why narrow their exposure to just two or three of the intelligences (even if those happen to be the ones more appreciated by our culture) if we can expose them to all seven? In the chart below **(The Seven Intelligences)**, we look at each of the intelligences in terms of ways to provide experiences for children that stimulate each intelligence and increase the potential for developing it.

THE SEVEN INTELLIGENCES

Intelligence	Opportunities for Stimulation at Home
Verbal/Linguistic	Reading to your children; listening to them read; encouraging them to keep diaries, journals, or travelogues; writing letters, such as thank-you letters for gifts; telling stories; listening to their stories; being playful with words (jokes,

Logical/ Mathematical	puns, nonsense words) Providing toys that involve patterns and shapes; engaging in problem-solving activities and games; encouraging simple math processes during the course of daily activities (shopping at the grocery store, for example); designing a recycling program for the home
Visual/Spatial	Providing basic building, designing, coloring, painting, and sculpting materials; encouraging child's own decorating of room; creating family calendars and chore charts
Body/Kinesthetic	Engaging in movement activities such as dancing, roller skating, tumbling, and play-wrestling; playing games that involve movement such as sports activities and dramatic interpretation
Musical/Rhythmic	Playing musical games using hand and body movements along with song ("patty cake," skipping rope, bouncing on the knee while singing); playing musical games that involve humming, whistling, tapping, and other playful sounds; making up playful songs to communicate ideas; playing a wide variety of music in the home
Interpersonal	Practicing effective communication skills, particularly listening, empathizing, and sharing

(continued)

(The Seven Intelligences—continued)

Intelligence	Opportunities for Stimulation at Home
Interpersonal	thoughts; doing household activities together as a team; allowing children to speak for themselves rather than speaking for them; treating children as real people when in conversation with other adults; respecting their feelings, opinions, and moods
Intrapersonal	Respecting, encouraging, and answering children's "why" questions; engaging in "what if" activities; modeling self-discipline; encouraging diaries to record emotions, feelings, and thoughts; providing spiritual activities such as meditating and praying

Providing a full range of activities for children through which they can maximize their exposure to the diversity of intelligences is clearly a tall order. But note that in the recommendations given above, none demands the purchase of expensive materials or the expenditure of special school tuition or the hiring of nannies or any other major material commitment. (And note the absence of any reference to TV!)

What they all do require is a healthy interest in and involvement with children. This involvement does not mean "planning their every activity," but, instead, simply being with them and giving them focused attention.

Exposing children to the fullest range of intelligences possible requires creative involvement with them—reading to them; playing spatial games with them; using building blocks with them; molding clay with them; coloring with them; singing songs with them; making up stories with them; and respectfully acknowledging their "why" questions. Doing these things will not only stimulate the widest possible range of intelligences, but will affirm them as special people worthy of time, attention, and recognition of their uniqueness.

> ## School-Smart Parenting Tip:
> **Provide simple, natural experiences for children that encompass the range of intelligences to expand their interests and discover and enhance their unique talents.**

Following the insights of Howard Gardner and his disciple David Lazear, Daniel Goleman, in his 1995 bestseller *Emotional Intelligence,* argues that our ability to handle our emotions and respond appropriately to them is an "intelligence" that has largely gone unappreciated. How many of us know individuals who, despite high levels of traditionally measured intelligence (high scores on the Stanford-Binet Intelligence Scale, SATs in the 1500s, straight "A's" in calculus), appear unsuccessful in dealing effectively with the "real world"? These folks may be strong in verbal and mathematical intelligence, but they are weak, argues Goleman, in emotional intelligence.

Goleman identifies five components of emotional intelligence. Once again, try to identify your children's particular strengths as we briefly review these qualities:

- Being **aware** of your own emotions—the ability to self-assess or identify and accept our feelings ("I am angry because Robert took my ball.")
- Being able to **manage** your emotions—the ability to make appropriate choices in response to our

feelings ("I have choices in how I respond to Robert for taking my ball; I can choose to hit him, or I can go tell the teacher, or I can talk to him, or . . .")

- Being able to **motivate** yourself—the ability to place needs over wants to accomplish goals ("I'd rather just hit Robert, but that is not the right thing to do so I will talk to him instead.")

- Recognizing emotions in others—the ability to **read feedback** from others ("I can see that Robert was angry with me for not playing with him and maybe that's why he took my ball.")

- Handling relationships—the ability to **respond effectively** to emotions in others ("Maybe if I play with Robert he will be happy and not angry with me anymore.")

Probably the most effective ways to teach these components of emotional intelligence is, first, to model them in our own lives; second, to provide specific real-life opportunities for children to practice them in their lives; and third, to actively affirm children for their efforts in each category.

The following chart (**Components of Emotional Intelligence**) offers specific suggestions for how to accomplish this:

COMPONENTS OF EMOTIONAL INTELLIGENCE

Emotion	Opportunities for Modeling and Practice
Awareness	**Owning** our own emotions through "I" statements ("I am angry about the mess in the bathroom because it was just cleaned and now there is water all over the floor.");

	allowing and respecting the child's emotions through empathy ("I can understand being afraid of the dark. I can remember being afraid of the dark too.")
Managing Emotions	**Waiting** before responding when angry; using time out, both for ourselves and for our children; asking "What else could you have done . . . ?" instead of "Why did you do that?"
Motivation	**Sharing** personal goals with your children; helping them break down long-term goals into smaller, manageable parts; giving allowances to encourage opportunities for them to make their own choices in buying things; avoiding rescuing; allowing natural consequences; applying logical consequences
Recognizing Emotions	**Respecting** emotions in others ("Your mother is very upset right now because of the mess in the bathroom. This is not the time to ask her when dinner will be ready."); avoiding attempts to forcefully change emotions ("Stop crying right now and enjoy the movie with the rest of the family.")

(continued)

(Components of Emotional Intelligence—continued)

Emotion	Opportunities for Modeling and Practice
Handling Relationships	**Responding** respectfully to others' emotions by actively acknowledging them ("Since Mom is so upset about the way the bathroom was left, why don't we start dinner for her."); avoiding the temptation to problem solve for another or "should have" for another ("You ruined your new dress because you pressed down too hard with the iron. What you should have done is . . .")

When parents take ownership of their feelings through "I" statements, practice time out, defer gratification, and respond effectively to other's emotions . . . they model emotional intelligence for children and provide opportunities for them to grow in their ability to work more effectively with feelings and respond appropriately to others.

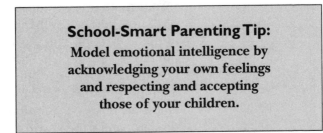

School-Smart Parenting Tip:
Model emotional intelligence by acknowledging your own feelings and respecting and accepting those of your children.

The process of affirming children includes openness, appreciation, and respect for the different ways they express their intelligence. This can be demonstrated in many ways.

In a touching scene from the pilot movie that introduced the television series *The Waltons,* John, the father, returns home on Christmas Eve with small gifts for each of the children. In presenting his gift to John-Boy, a sensitive child who loved to write, John confessed that, although he couldn't understand his son's love for writing, he bought him this gift to support his efforts.

The gift—Big Chief writing tablets—was the last thing the father would want for himself, but the best gift that John-Boy could receive. John may not have understood his son's verbal/linguistic intelligence, but (unlike the parents in *Dead Poets' Society,* who gave their son the same desk set for every birthday), he respected it enough to provide his son an outlet for that talent.

When we appreciate that each child is talented and gifted in unique ways and seek to understand the unique mode of intelligence that he or she possesses, we demonstrate respect. We give concrete expression to that respect when we give them gifts, on special occasions, that reflect their talents; we encourage them to organize their space (particularly their rooms) to reflect their own interests; and we engage them in conversation about those interests. In doing so, we provide them the opportunity to more fully understand their strengths.

Exposing children to the multiple intelligences and opportunities to develop their emotional intelligence is particularly important in their early years. When we place young children in front of the television all day, we encourage them to become passive participants in their worlds.

By contrast, when we offer them opportunities to actively fashion their world with blocks and boxes and string and clay, provide a diverse home environment, and model emotional maturity when they are very young, they are more likely to approach their school years with an attitude of active involvement. The resultant diversity of interests and emotional maturity will surely serve them well.

Positive Expectations

What about expectations? Is it not true that study after study has demonstrated that a teacher's or parent's expectations will affect a child's achievement? If so, how does this square with our temptation to hold our children up in comparison to the models of success in our minds, rather than to encourage them to fulfill their own unique potential?

The classic study on the effect of expectations on students took place in 1968 under Harvard professors Robert Rosenthal and Lenore Jacobsen. Taking two similar groups of elementary school children, labeling one group as gifted (using their locker numbers, which were numbered in the 120s, to assign them fake IQ scores) and the other group as average, Rosenthal and Jacobsen discovered that the children labeled as gifted did in fact excel in school, regardless of their actual IQ scores.

They noticed that teachers gave the "gifted" students more opportunities to answer questions and more time to answer them. They addressed them more often by name, and stepped closer to and touched them more often. The teachers' high expectations of the students affected how they treated them and how the students performed in response. This is powerful information for teachers and parents alike.

More recently, positive expectations have been celebrated in the motion picture *Stand and Deliver,* a story about East Los Angeles high school math teacher Jaime Escalante, who galvanized a group of ghetto kids into becoming advanced placement calculus scholars.

In a biography that followed the success of the motion picture, *Escalante: The Best Teacher in America* (Henry Holt) by Jay Mathews, the story is told of Henry Gradillas, Garfield High School biology teacher during the 1970s and a role model for Escalante. Gradillas, troubled by the absence of positive expectations among many of his fellow teachers and many of the students, quietly embarked on an experiment to test the power of expectations.

Students in two basic biology classes, which contained similar students divided randomly, were told, in the one class, that they were college material with much potential and, in the other class, that they were lazy and there was little hope for them. Giving more difficult tests and more homework to the first group and just the minimum to the second, his expectations proved true . . . in both cases.

During the first quarter, the first group lived up to Gradillas' expectations by mastering a college-level biology test; the second lived down to his expectations by producing only one "A," with 30 percent of the class getting "D's" and "F's." Doing his best to salvage the rest of the year by communicating positive expectations for both, Gradillas never managed to compensate fully for the effects of the initial expectations on the second group.

Positive expectations became the rallying cry for Jaime Escalante; his success (and the success of many who hold high expectations for their students) demonstrates the importance of this principle: "Positive expectations, when grounded in respect for the unique potential of young people, can have profound, lasting effects."

But two cautions need to be expressed here. First, parents need to avoid the barrier of expecting too much too soon, as was discussed in chapter 2, "Barriers and Builders." Remember that progress comes in steps, sometimes very small steps. When we celebrate any effort being made toward that progress, we effectively communicate high expectations.

> **School-Smart Parenting Tip:**
> We affirm children best when we
> *communicate* (through our attitude,
> words, and behavior) *positive expectations*
> *for their accomplishment.*

Secondly, unrealistic expectations, expectations that do not respect the specific talents and capabilities of children, may discourage them. Adults who tell children that they can succeed at anything in life if they just keep trying do them a disservice.

As we have already discussed, each child has a range of abilities in any number of areas; practice, commitment, and positive expectations enable each child to test the outer limits of his or her range. Our challenge is to be open to children's unique talents, intelligences, interests, and hobbies; communicate to them our unwavering belief in their potential; and acknowledge the progress that results from their efforts.

A Child's Room: A Personal Space

One very important area in which we can communicate to children that they are worthy of respect is their personal space. The degree to which we encourage children to see their rooms as expressions of themselves will have a direct impact on their sense of self.

This includes the issue of what requirements we will make for the care and cleanliness of that room. The degree to which children perceive their rooms as personal space is the degree to which they are willing to respect it and work in it. All children need places they can call their own, that are their domain and their responsibility.

Parents are well advised to allow children's rooms to be places they can decorate as they wish; places where they can enjoy their own music; places of privacy that others (including parents) do not, under normal circumstances, enter against their wishes. There are limits to this, of course. After all, the child's room is part of our house and the child is part of the family with responsibilities to that family. He or she needs to develop an understanding of what that means.

The limits we as parents set are most effective when we design them to teach respect for, and inclusion in, the *whole* family . . . rather than use them to control the child. By using family meetings to establish basic responsibilities and limits, we will encourage children to take ownership for them.

This discussion applies just as well to situations in which children have to share bedrooms. Such children have the opportunity to learn cooperation as they work out issues regarding space, decorating, privacy, cleanliness, noise level, and so on. Parents are well advised to encourage children to work out these issues themselves, and to interfere as little as possible.

A good test for evaluating your approach to the issue of children's rooms might be to honestly consider these questions: Are my decisions being made for the child's benefit . . . or for my own? Am I looking out for my own interests more than for those of my child? Am I trying to look good to the neighbors, or to be effective as a parent? Am I trying to fulfill my need for perfection (or someone else's need for perfection), or am I helping my child develop standards of his or her own? Are the rules and limits my way of controlling my child's life, or helping him learn to control his own life? Am I truly looking out for my child's interests and needs for personal space?

A helpful rule of thumb might be: When dealing with children's rooms, allow them more freedom than you would allow for the rest of the house. Although you can't stand to leave your own bed unmade, how important is it that your children make their beds every day? If it is important to you, then make that your rule. If not, establish another requirement, such as: Make beds once a week, or at least when company is coming. (A friend who works in parent education puts it simply to those who take her classes: "You don't like the way your child's room looks? Close the door!")

Affirmation and Healthy Self-Esteem

The importance of self-esteem cannot be overemphasized. But what is it? Where does it come from? What are its limitations? Healthy self-esteem is not arrogance or self-centeredness; it is, instead, this perception: "I am worthy of dignity and respect, not because of anything I have done or not done, but just because I am."

Self-esteem does not come from others' praise, well-meaning though it may be, or from gold stars that teachers place on papers. It emerges from experiences, both positive and negative, through which we gain wisdom and learn that we are capable, significant people who make choices that influence our lives.

Recycling an old saying, it might not be too simplistic to say that your self-esteem ends where my self-esteem begins. If my self-esteem encourages me to go out into the world with confidence and be of service to others, it is healthy. If it leads me to believe and act as though the entire world revolves around my every want and need, it can be quite unhealthy.

A New York Minute!

Several years ago, a new mayor of New York City was inaugurated in a much-publicized, media-highlighted, and, ultimately, very embarrassing ceremony. With his ten-year-old son standing next to him, the new mayor began his inauguration speech.

To the embarrassment of all (except, so it appeared, to the mayor himself) and to the delight of the late-night talk shows that satirized the event during subsequent weeks, the young son proceeded to mimic his father's words, mug the camera, and gesture theatrically, all to a national television audience.

The boy behaved as one who was raised to believe that his wants and needs predominate over everything else. He behaved as one whose self-esteem is so high that the needs of the rest of the world (for solemnity and formality, not to mention plain good manners, in that case) don't count.

"High" vs. "Healthy"

For years we have heard that self-esteem is the most important issue in parenting, that by focusing on raising our children's self-esteem, everything else will work out just fine. However, it is possible to have such high, unhealthy self-esteem that we live a life of delusion. It is also possible to have low, healthy self-esteem and be living a life of humility.

If our current understanding of self-esteem doesn't translate to respect for the needs of others and realistic assessment of one's own behavior, then the issue of self-esteem needs review.

And it is finally receiving review. Thanks to critical thinkers like Alfie Kohn, author of *Punished by Rewards: The Trouble with Gold Stars, Incentive Plans, A's, Praise, and Other Bribes,* the whole self-esteem movement is being subjected to closer inspection. In a December 1994 article in the professional education journal *Kappan,* Kohn summarizes his concern about the direction the self-esteem movement has taken in these jarringly honest words: "*I'm special, I'm* important, here's how *I* feel about things. The whole enterprise could be said to encourage a self-absorption bordering on narcissism.*"*

Those schooled in the issues surrounding self-esteem have long questioned the direction of the self-esteem movement in America. Two concerns regarding the directions the movement has taken are of particular note.

The first, identified by Kohn in the above quote, concerns the egocentric nature of the vocabulary of self-esteem. *I'm* special; *I'm* important. How important is it that we reinforce this with children and students? Kohn asks. Would it not be healthier to teach that we are *all* special, we are *all* important?

Of course, both concepts are important. Perhaps the central question is: Is it possible to deemphasize the latter in our enthusiasm to promote the former? The example of the new mayor's son suggests that this may be happening.

The second concern, identified by many commentators on the issue, revolves around the source of self-esteem. When their sense of self is primarily developed externally (as a result of approval given by others or achieving things others value, for example), people become dependent on others and on circumstances for their sense of well-being. When sense of self is developed internally (the result of risks taken, hardships endured, personal goals met, and a sense of self-respect and self-efficacy), people can transcend the approval of others and the effects of circumstances to create their own sense of well-being.

Since the latter is clearly the healthiest and most desirable, what role do adults play in providing activities, opportunities, and challenges for young people through which they can develop healthy self-esteem? What does this view say about the wisdom of allowing children to experience discomfort and even failure so they can learn to rise above adversity, build a better plan, and develop confidence in their own resources for overcom-ing difficulty?

Kohn and others argue that if we really want to help our children feel good about themselves, we should always treat them with respect, rather than shower them with praise. After all, what does the word "esteem" mean? It is a synonym for "respect." Self-esteem is, therefore, largely a product or reflection of self-respect.

Just as we teach responsibility by giving children responsibilities, we teach self-respect by giving our children respect. When children are treated with respect and are affirmed for their efforts to face challenges and show respect for others, the result is healthy self-esteem.

Birth Order

In *The Birth Order Book* (DTP), author Kevin Leman relates the following statistics about firstborns:

- Of the first twenty-three astronauts sent into outer space, twenty-one were firstborns.
- All seven astronauts in the original Mercury pro-gram were firstborns.
- More than half the United States presidents were firstborns.
- Firstborns are over-represented among *Who's Who in America* and *American Men and Women of Science,* as well as among Rhodes scholars and university professors.

Get the picture? Firstborns tend to be highly moti-vated to achieve. They tend to be analytical, organized, and precise; and they thrive on structure and order. First-born children are likely to spend hours sorting baseball cards, meticulously furnishing a dollhouse, playing school (with the firstborn as the teacher and her friends the students), organizing stamp and coin collections, strategically positioning the latest action figures around the room, bossing other children in the neighborhood, and generally behaving more adult-like than other children in the family. Why is this likely to be the case?

The bottom line is that children tend to develop according to their perceptions of their parents' expectations and treatment of them . . . and/or their older siblings expectations and treatment of them. Birth order is a major factor in those expectations and treatment. Firstborns tend to get a lot of adult attention, and have a lot expected of them. They are often expected to justify their parents before the world. Adults are initially the child's only models. Firstborns generally perceive this and respond accordingly.

> ### School-Smart Parenting Tip:
> **Promote healthy self-esteem by showing respect for children and their abilities and encouraging them to respect themselves and others.**

Second-born children, particularly those of the same sex as the firstborn, generally experience very different expectations from the parents. Even when parents try to expect the same of the second as of the firstborn child, the second-born tends to perceive things very differently. Second children often perceive that the firstborn has carved out a little niche for himself, the niche of the little adult who does everything right and whose first tooth and first step and first words and first smile are all dutifully celebrated, communicated, and recorded for posterity by the parents. (Look at most family photograph albums!)

The second-born often perceives that he or she must find significance somewhere other than the places the firstborn found it. There has already been a first tooth, step, word, smile, and so on. So these children must look for another way to be noticed, get attention, and feel significant. Sometimes they find it in rebellion or at least through trying to be the opposite of the firstborn.

If the firstborn was Mr. Do-Whatever-Mom-and-Dad-Want (because they will clap and celebrate and call all the aunts and uncles when the child does what they want), then the second-born may try to do whatever Mom and Dad *don't* want to get the attention that would otherwise be denied by following the pattern of the firstborn. After all, doing whatever Mom and Dad want, which has already been done by the firstborn, is no longer any big deal.

Let's say a third son comes along. Third son has two older siblings as role models for his own development. He perceives that they are very different, if for no other reason than that they are always fighting. He notices that they fight with each other, not with him. Often, he concludes that his role is that of peacemaker, mediator. His perception is: "My role in this family is to bring peace between my older brothers."

Let's continue this not-so-hypothetical birth-order picture a little further. One year after third-born son comes a daughter—the firstborn daughter. Because she has three older brothers ahead of her, she must fight to survive. She must learn to use her wits and her words and her strength of character if she is to fend off the buffets of her older siblings. She also perceives that there is no space in which to become a privileged only daughter or a taken-care-of last-born because two years later comes . . . a second-born daughter.

Daughter number two enters a home rapidly approaching chaos. Firstborn son and second-born son are in constant conflict. Third-born son is running around trying to mediate between them or shift attention away from them. Firstborn daughter is becoming toughened and hardened and just a little bossy as she learns various ways to fend off her brothers' criticisms, insults, and bullying.

The second-born daughter often perceives that the role of diplomat/caretaker is still available. Her role is to mediate this mess, to bring peace. Her role is to cry out, in the midst of all this turmoil, "Can't we all just love each other?" It is no surprise that second-born daughter often becomes best friends with, and a caretaker for, the third-born son (the first family mediator, the role model of mediators).

Hopefully, you begin to get a feeling for the complexity of birth order. It is important to note that, while birth order influences probabilities and supports limited stereotyping, it is not a very reliable predictor because far too many variables are at work.

Like personality and intelligence styles, birth order does not define, but it does help to describe. First-borns and only children do tend to be more responsible, achievement-oriented, perfectionistic, and leadership oriented; middle children do tend more often than not to be mediators, diplomats, and caretakers; and last-born children tend to achieve less, be less perfectionistic, and rely more on personal charm.

It is helpful for parents to recognize the qualities children are likely to demonstrate as a result of birth order, maximize the positive aspects of those qualities, and assist children in compensating for any negative aspects. The challenge is to treat them all fairly but not necessarily the same, recognizing that each child has different needs. The chart on page 179 **(Birth-Order Resolutions)** offers specific examples of techniques we can use to meet this challenge:

BIRTH-ORDER RESOLUTIONS	
Birth Order	Parenting Opportunities
First Child	Encourage and provide opportunities for her to be with her own age group; share your own imperfections with her; avoid "fixing" her jobs (straightening out the covers on the bed she just made, for example); be a "good finder" by focusing on what she did right and minimizing what she did wrong; allow some special privileges to compensate for the special responsibilities she will have; remember to give her one-on-one time, especially when that second child comes along
Second Child	Accept the differences of the second child; be attuned to different interests, talents, and needs; recognize and acknowledge his "firsts"; avoid comparisons; give one-on-one time
Middle Child	Be attuned to the middle child's need to be seen as someone special; avoid overdoing the hand-me-downs; be sure to continue whatever activities you engaged in for the older children (such as baby pictures, photo albums, drawings posted on the refrigerator, music lessons); provide special responsibilities and privileges; give one-on-one time

(continued)

(Birth-Order Resolutions—continued)

Birth Order	Parenting Opportunities
Last Child	Avoid "doing for" and discourage the older children from "doing for"; be especially attuned to providing chores and responsibilities around the house and enforcing family rules; recognize accomplishments; maintain the photo album and post those drawings; give one-on-one time
Only Child	Remember that the parents' most important job is to prepare the child for the day he will leave the nest and fly on his own; allow the child to make mistakes and learn from them; avoid giving too much and preventing the child from earning things on his own; provide opportunities for mixing with other children, and for sharing and compromising; make sure you, the parents, are the center of the home and that you have a life of your own—get a babysitter and go out by yourselves

(For a more complete discussion of birth order see *The Birth Order Book* referenced on page 175.)

The more we understand about birth order, the more prepared we are to recognize the behaviors that tend to be associated with each position in the family, and the more prepared we will be to help children maximize their personal assets and minimize their liabilities.

"Is My Child Ready for School?"

The law says that children are eligible to enter kindergarten when they are five years old by September 1 (or whatever the date in your state). However, to be eligible is not necessarily to be ready! Readiness does not have a specific timetable.

Readiness is best determined developmentally rather than chronologically. Just as no two children take their first steps at the same age, no two of them will be developmentally ready for schooling at exactly the same time. Unfortunately, we often expect them to be ready just because they have turned five, which is, all too frequently, not necessarily the case. How does a parent know if the child should go to kindergarten or, instead, stay home for another year of maturation?

Pediatricians, teachers, school counselors, and your own experience can all help here. There are also some specific clues. If you have concerns that your child may not be ready for kindergarten, use this checklist as a guide:

- Is she comfortable being away from home and her parents for several hours each day?
- Can he take care of his bathroom and hygiene responsibilities?
- Can she express herself—her needs, her concerns, her ideas, her feelings—to other adults and children?
- Has he demonstrated the ability to try new things and engage in new activities without undue fear?
- Can she handle her emotions well?
- Can he work well with other children his own age?
- Can she work independently?

- Does he take care of his belongings?
- Does she respect the belongings of others?
- Can he do simple drawings that are recognizable?
- Is her physical coordination in line with other children her age?
- Does pencil control result in firm strokes or wobbly strokes?

Note that this question was not on the list: Does she demonstrate advanced verbal skills? That is because it is *not* a reliable indicator of readiness! Demonstrating advanced verbal skills, which is common for firstborns, is more an indicator that the child is surrounded by adults rather than by other children. Remember that firstborn children have mostly Mom and Dad for models, including models for their verbal skills.

If discussions with pediatricians, teachers, and counselors; your own experience and wisdom; and the checklist above lead you to have doubts about your child's readiness, it's probably better to wait a year. ("When in doubt, keep her out!") A child has plenty of time to savor life's experiences, and being held out a year for developmental readiness will not set him or her back.

On the other hand, pushing children before they are ready may cause them frustration throughout their school years. Starting too soon often results in the child's chronically low achievement and feelings of inadequacy and not "fitting in." Objectively consider all the above before enrolling a child in kindergarten. This first specific, school-related decision for most parents is an important one.

Clearly, there is a lot to the issue of affirming children. Perhaps the best way to sum it up is to emphasize again that each child is unique. Each has a world distinct from that of parents and siblings.

By recognizing and validating their worlds, we affirm children's uniqueness. By offering recognition, support,

School-Smart Parenting Tip:
Avoid the temptation to rush children
into school; instead, look seriously
at the readiness question and . . .
if in doubt, keep them out!

and encouragement as they develop, we enable our children to experience school with more excitement, enthusiasm, and investment, and increase their repertoire of interests and talents.

▼

Chapter

14

Emotional Stability

The wild things roared their terrible roars
and gnashed their terrible teeth
and rolled their terrible eyes and showed their terrible claws
but Max stepped into his private boat and waved good-bye
and sailed back over a year
and in and out of weeks
and through a day
and into the night of his very own room
where he found his supper waiting for him
and it was still hot.

—Where the Wild Things Are, *Maurice Sendak*

The third asset of highly effective families is a home environment characterized by emotional stability. Such families have learned to create a safe and supportive oasis where children can test their strengths and weaknesses. This helps them build and maintain confidence for the school years and avoid the pressures that often result from emotional instability in the family.

An October 1993 issue of *USA Today* featured an article describing a survey of adolescents designed to determine the factors that led to success in school. According to the survey, what correlated most directly with high achievement and healthy self-esteem was *not* socioeconomic status, race, or ethnicity; whether the school was public or private; whether the school was located in an affluent neighborhood or in a poor neighborhood; family make-up; or any of the factors we readily (and carelessly) assume to be predictive of success. The one factor that correlated most with achievement in school was whether or not the family sat down to eat dinner *together* on a regular basis.

In a 1995 study undertaken by the publishers of *Who's Who Among American High School Seniors,* the 1993 findings reported in *USA Today* were confirmed. Based on responses from 3,351 young people in their teenage years, the study revealed that young people who regularly share meals with their families are three times more likely to say that their home life is happy and their relationship with their parents is close.

Sitting down with the family and eating dinner together on a regular basis—what a wonderful advantage for parents! Teachers can't do that with their students (although regular class meetings might produce many similar benefits). But parents can do it, thereby providing a safe, comfortable, repeatable setting in which children can experience community and develop as healthy young people.

Michael was giving a presentation not long ago on the subject of raising children for success and happiness in school. A young mother of three children, the oldest of whom would be starting school within a few months, interrupted his comments with the direct challenge: "Okay, so just what do I need to do to ensure that my children will be successful in school?"

"Do you really want to know?" Michael asked.

"Yes," she shot back, "enough of all this introductory stuff. Just tell me what I need to do."

He answered, "Well, if you really want your children to experience success and happiness in school . . ." (then he dramatically paused and scanned the audience, making eye contact with as many as he could) ". . . what you really need to do is sit down with them and eat dinner together on a regular basis."

She did not hide her disappointment, but he let the answer hang in the air nonetheless. Finally, she said, with undisguised frustration: "Sit down and eat dinner together? *That's* what I drove all the way out here today to hear?"

After a few moments, Michael did what experienced speakers do when challenged by an audience participant . . . he involved the whole audience in problem solving. He threw the issue out to them and challenged them to come up with reasons why sitting down together for dinner could impact a child's emotional stability, and thereby lead to success in school. With the audience involved, he was soon able to fill in the picture with a broader perspective on the importance of providing a home environment characterized by emotional stability.

He did not do that to frustrate the questioner, although she probably felt otherwise. He did it for emphasis, hoping that his point would remain with the listeners long after other points made during the presentation were forgotten.

In our fast-paced, over-involved, over-scheduled, stress-filled world, there are truly few things that parents can provide for children that are better than thirty to forty-five minutes with them. Sitting around the dinner table, passing the potatoes and sharing thoughts, concerns, and experiences of the day makes a particularly strong statement of family priorities when the TV is off and the telephone recorder is on.

The Influence of Family Life on the Child

The dinner table may be the perfect metaphor for the renewal of family life, which is a critical factor in improving our schools. We once heard a speaker, a hardened man who had spent a great deal of his life in prison ministry, talk about the death of the American family. His statistics were chilling: So many more fatherless homes, so many more unwed pregnant teenagers, so many more cases of spousal abuse, so many more cases of child abuse, and on and on. It was a gloomy picture.

His prescription, however, was even gloomier. Since the American family is dead, we need to provide other models to replace it; the churches, community organizations, and the local, state, and federal governments must step up to the plate and offer themselves as alternatives to the family.

Michael could not resist challenging this prescription. After thanking the presenter and recognizing a few good points he had made, Michael took his gloves off and started swinging with both fists.

There can be no alternative to the American family, he responded. Not the churches, not community organizations, and not—God help us!—the government! (He found himself standing at this point.) The American family is alive and well! Many of them, as we speak, are sitting down together around the dinner table, sharing their joys and frustrations and passing the potatoes! There *is* hope for America!

He sat back down. The speaker looked at him, hesitated, and said, "Thank you so much for sharing." Others in the audience started discreetly moving away from Michael, who looked around for the nearest exit.

As humorous as that was, the point remains: There is no alternative to the family. Which of all the institutions that affect us has the greatest influence on the child? Where do we need to focus our attention if we are going to strengthen our schools . . . and our children?

Just how important is the influence of the family on the child? Dr. Kevin Leman, who popularized Alfred Adler's theories on birth order and its effects on a child's perception of his family role in *The Birth Order Book,* argues forcefully that a child's family exerts more influence on him than any other system, organization, institution, or even experience that he might have in life.

As the world becomes more hectic and fast-paced, more confusing and technologically overpowering, the steadying influence of the family is ever more essential. When all else is confusing and confounding, the family at home remains the one true constant that can be counted on to be there . . . around the table eating dinner together, sharing the experiences of the day, listening to each others' joys and frustrations, passing the potatoes.

The Family Dinner

Sitting around the table eating dinner together—a prescription so simple that we are tempted to minimize its importance. But to do so would be a serious mistake. Schedule an hour, if possible, for the family dinner. Avoid the temptation to run from the table as soon as the dishes are cleared. Leave the TV off. (According to a survey reported in *National Times,* September 1995, 66 percent of Americans regularly eat dinner while watching TV. So much for dinnertime communication!) Let the telephone recorder pick up those irresistible offers for new credit cards and alternative long-distance services, and the opportunities to contribute to favorite charities.

In families for which nightly dinner together is an impossibility due to conflicting work schedules, soccer practices, or meetings, choose one or two nights a week to keep free from outside distractions and make them special dinnertimes. Even if only once a week, that special dinnertime together or a regular brunch on the weekend can go a long way to providing emotional stability in the family.

Some families that must limit shared dinnertimes have ways to make even just one night very special. Some eat at the formal dinner table, with the guests-only dinnerware, a few candles burning, soft music in the background, and a full meal served leisurely.

The key is to use the family meal as an opportunity to bring all family members together in a relaxed setting with as few distractions as possible. By doing so, we communicate to family members that they are more important than television, outside schedules, people on the other end of the telephone, and so on.

Of course, as children grow up and peers become a larger and larger part of their world, they may not want to linger at the table as long as parents would like. That's okay. Let them go ahead and leave early. Show understanding for their developing personhood.

Most importantly, stay at the table with the other family members for the full mealtime and keep the family dinner going. Nothing will provide a safer and more secure harbor for young people than knowing that, when they do wish to linger (as they will from time to time), we are still there . . . sitting around the table . . . passing the potatoes.

Family Time

Dad's job keeps him working late four nights a week, Monday through Thursday. Mom has part-time work outside the home, a full carpool schedule before and after, and the cooking to do at the end of the day. (The other family chores are divided as equally as possible among all family members; this family has already read chapter 12, "A Family of Contributors.") Friday night is reserved for Mom and Dad together, and on Saturday nights the kids get involved with their friends on a fairly regular basis. So Sunday is reserved as the one time the family can eat together. It is also reserved as family time.

Many families extend the family meal into a family night. This simply means one night set aside weekly for the family to be available to one another for an extended period of time—playing games, telling stories, reading to each other, making a dessert together, doing projects together, planning outings and vacations, and such. Like the family meal, a scheduled family night is one more opportunity to communicate to children that they are worth time and attention. It clearly demonstrates that they are more important than all the distractions of the world.

Family nights can be enhanced by allowing children to choose and/or plan an activity, ensuring variation in activities, and throwing in surprises from time to time (a trip to an ice cream shop, for example). A key is to schedule it and stick with it, like the family meal. Later, when the teenagers start drifting away, keep on doing it anyway. When they do drift back, they will appreciate the little oasis you continue to provide in family night.

One final note: Don't forget one-on-one time with the children. As positive an experience as having the entire family together is, there is something extra special about keeping a date with each child individually. Few interactions more effectively promote one's perception of being an important member than when a community head (in this case Mom or Dad) seeks one member out for special attention. Most people vividly remember times when they had one parent's undivided attention. It's a powerful communicator of significance, well worth the time it takes.

Family Meetings

A weekly meeting can provide a structured and somewhat formal opportunity for the family to get together and communicate. This might well be the most effective means of ensuring that all family members will be affirmed as significant, contributing members of the household. Family meetings can be structured to allow each family member, children as well as adults, to participate in family decision making.

Family meetings provide opportunities for sharing both joys and disappointments, giving compliments and thanks, speaking and listening. They provide a forum for working out difficulties, distributing responsibility for chores, discussing changes in family routines, and planning activities and vacations.

The mechanics of the family meeting need not be complicated. Simply stated, it is a weekly meeting attended by all family members to share interests and concerns and discuss family issues. Many families provide a written agenda in advance, to which each family member can add items for discussion.

This agenda might be a sheet of paper posted on the refrigerator, a shoebox with a slot cut in the top, or any convenient means to allow members to write down items of concern. Other families simply give each member a chance to speak rather than following a formal agenda. In any case, every family member who wishes to contribute should be allowed time to do so.

The setting for the family meeting might use a format similar to the following:

- A chairperson is appointed to keep the meeting on task. If possible, each family member should have a turn at being chairperson.
- Each family member is encouraged to share one positive thing that happened to him or her during the past week. This helps to set a tone of positive expectations, countering the complaining that often mars family discussions. In addition, each member is encouraged to compliment or give thanks to another family member. This is important because it provides an atmosphere of support where discussion can take place openly, and differences of opinion will have a greater chance of being addressed as problems to be worked out rather than challenges to the relationship. When you sincerely compliment me or thank me for something specific I have done, I am more willing to listen to you and consider your point of view.
- The first agenda item is read and the family member who placed it on the agenda is asked whether this is still a concern. (Or, if no formal agenda has been posted, each family member takes turns bringing up matters for discussion.) If the item is no longer a concern, the next agenda item is chosen. (Interestingly, many items placed on the agenda during the week are no longer a problem come family meeting day. The very act of writing the problem down often serves as a release of anger, which might be all that is needed. Also, some time has passed, and time, though it can not heal all wounds, does heal many of them.)
- If the agenda item is still a problem, the family member who raised the issue is asked what solution she thinks might best address it. After this, all other family members are allowed to offer their solutions. Brainstorming is a particularly effective way to get ideas on the table at this point. A solution is chosen, preferably by consensus

rather than majority rule (which tends to polarize), and the next item is addressed. When all issues have been addressed, the family might celebrate with a special dessert, story time, or game.

Why the structure and formality? In another time, in another place, there was probably no need for formal, structured family meetings. Today, however, when family members often race off in all different directions, rarely sit down together to talk, frequently compete with TV and other technologies as barriers to dialogue, and face stresses and pressures unknown a generation ago, we may well need to intervene in a formal, structured way.

We may, in fact, need to create a family culture to compensate for the society in which we live. Ensuring that at least once a week all family members have a chance to be listened to and affirmed may require planning and organization. The structure noted above need not be followed strictly. What is important is that we take time to ensure that some format exists for family sharing. Otherwise, we may not have a process for learning what is on each other's minds.

One family, for example, uses a powerful teaching aid, the Talking Stick, at their family meetings. The Talking Stick, which originates from Native American tribes in the Great Plains region, is simply a stick—maybe a foot and a half to two feet long, decorated as desired with feathers, strips of leather, and beads. It is held by the family meeting participant whose turn it is to talk. As long as the family member has the stick, she can talk without being interrupted.

The Talking Stick does far more than allow the holder to speak. While the holder of the stick is talking, the other family members must be listening. In fact, the next person who wishes to speak may not do so until he or she repeats back to the previous speaker what was said, to the speaker's satisfaction. Only when the first person is satisfied that he or she has been listened to will the next person be allowed to speak.

So the Talking Stick is also a Listening Stick. It encourages all meeting participants to listen carefully to the speaker, rather than plan what they want to say. The Talking Stick serves, then, as a physical reminder of how important listening is to respectful communication. What a public service it would be to send each member of Congress a Talking Stick!

A number of concerns need to be addressed if family meetings are to effectively and respectfully involve all family members:

• A participant in one of our parenting seminars during a discussion about family meetings once observed:

"We had family meetings when I was a kid. We all sat together around the dinner table with Dad at the head telling us what we were going to do, how we were going to do it, and when we were going to do it."

Clearly, that's not what we have in mind here. The purpose of the family meeting is to provide a process through which each family member can be heard, have his or her ideas thoughtfully considered, and be affirmed. It is not a format for parental directing.

• Neither is the family meeting an opportunity for kid-bashing. There is a place for adult correction of children's behavior, but it should be in private, in respect for the feelings of the child, not in the group setting of the family meeting. The family meeting should be a positive experience for all family members.

• The effective family meeting is one in which all family members know what is open for debate and what is not. The effective parent will ensure that items *not* open for debate are those that represent the basic family values and the rules that support them. The family meeting is not an abdication of parental responsibility. Providing a forum through which children can be listened to, considered, and affirmed does not mean that every idea they have is open to a family vote.

The effective family is one that has aligned itself with basic principles, such as respectfulness, honesty, courtesy, and truthfulness. Further, the family has made rules of conduct regarding such issues as curfews, television viewing, homework, and household chores. The family meeting may well provide a forum for the *discussion* of these items, but as responsibility ultimately lies with the parents, the decision must lie there as well.

School-Smart Parenting Tip:
Use family dinners, family meetings,
and family nights to provide a structure
and process in which children can
experience support, affirmation,
communication, and a sense of belonging.

Closing Time

No matter how hectic a day might have been, and no matter how many negative experiences may have occurred, ending that day on a peaceful, positive note can provide emotional stability. We cannot guarantee or ensure that children's days are filled with positive experiences. We can, however, make a concerted effort to end the day in a reassuring and supportive manner.

When children go to bed in peaceful surroundings, regardless of how the day they just completed went, they are more likely to be positive about the day to come. Send them to bed angry and alienated, and they tend to carry anger and alienation over into the new day.

Out of respect for this principle, many families have a designated "closing time," after which no more individual work is done and all family members can enjoy each other's company before it's time to turn out the lights and go to bed. Even if it's only fifteen minutes, and even if Mom and Dad still have more to do before the evening is over, setting aside time for children to be together with parents can be a pleasant and supportive way to end their day.

At closing time, homework, housework, and office work stops. The family comes together to close out the day with personal reflections, a story, a prayer, whatever best meets the family needs. Closing time helps to refocus on the family, to remind all family members that whatever has happened in each one's day, whatever directions each family member has taken, we now come together as a family to share time together.

Television Influences

Michael had a dream the other night that he was watching television and the opening scene of *Leave It to Beaver* was just coming on the screen. And there was The Beave, in black and white, walking home from school (*walking* home from school!), whistling in a happy and carefree manner, clicking a picket fence with a stick as he ambled along. If there were any troubles going on in the world, they were definitely not affecting The Beave.

Michael turned the dial *(turned the dial!)* and there appeared Andy Griffith as the sheriff and little Ron Howard as Opie strolling down a country lane together, fishing poles slung over their shoulders, with that so recognizable tune whistling in the background. If there were any problems in Mayberry, they were surely being put on hold for a day's fishing.

He turned the dial once again and there was Mary Tyler Moore, flipping her hat in the air, whistling the happiest of tunes (Why did everybody whistle so much back then?) and, like Sheriff Andy, Opie, and The Beave, she clearly had no care in the world.

Then Michael awoke. Hoping to prolong those pleasant memories and pursuing the fantasy that they just might linger if he wished for it hard enough, he rushed to the family room, picked up the remote, and started clicking away.

With the first click, a very expensive sports car came on the screen, screeching through dark, wet, urban streets. In just a second or two, it crashed against a wall and burst into flames, bodies constrained and helpless inside. A second car came to an abrupt stop and the driver pulled out a semiautomatic and pumped a clipful of bullets into the writhing bodies inside, just in case.

He clicked the remote just in time to catch a well-known family sitcom as the wife was berating the husband for his lack of sexual prowess. He in turn was attacking her for no longer having whatever had aroused that sexual prowess in earlier years.

Once again, he clicked . . . to a talk show on which the audience, at the host's baiting, screamed insults at a group of teenagers who were on the show because, as they complained, their parents never listen to them. The teenagers just sat there, shaking their heads as if to say, "See what we mean?"

Michael clicked once more and watched a victim of spousal abuse, her face still swollen from the latest attack, arguing in a panel discussion for stronger legislation against abusers. One more click and an advertisement for a top-selling beer tried to convince Michael that he would have a muscled, tanned, and youthful body if he consumed their product. At that point, Michael decided to go back to bed and "dream on!"

Has any single invention of the past fifty years had more influence on children than television? In 1954, the typical American household spent about three hours a day watching TV; in 1994, the average was up to seven. There are no signs this is decreasing, nor that we will be returning soon to the days of *Mayberry RFD*, where our only childhood restraint was getting home before dark. The computer has revolutionized the world of education, as well as the world of business; but its effect on young children, particularly those in the early years of schooling, is still minimal compared to television. This may change with the rapidly improving capabilities of the computer (including the increasing availability and potential of the Internet and similar services), but this will only result in a replacement of even greater influence—and no greater comfort for parents—than TV ever had.

In fact, the computer may not only replace the TV as the dominant technology in the home; it may very well totally supplant it, making TV, as a separate and distinct unit in the house, obsolete. When home videos start coming to us through the computer, will it be long before the TV and the computer become one unit, a mega-computer/TV/video store all in one? The prospects are at once awesome and frightening.

For now, television is clearly the dominant technological distraction for young children, and a very influential "teacher." This fact is of particular importance to parents of preschoolers, for whom the impact of television is greatest. Television is as familiar to children as the furniture in their home. In fact, in many homes televisions are the dominant pieces of furniture.

Was there life before television? What did people *do* back then? How did they entertain themselves? Believe it or not, there really was life before television and, risking oversimplification, it would be helpful to look at that life. Before TV dominated the family room, family members communicated. They discussed, played, gossiped . . . and, yes, argued, bickered, and fought. But there was communication.

Adults communicated. Children communicated. Through such dialogue, interpersonal skills were developed. Television drastically altered all that, resulting in family members interacting not with each other but with a box that grew to assume a status larger than any one of us, indeed larger than all of us put together. Television disrupted the most important language class in a child's life—family conversation.

Not content with the altering of family patterns that took place in the family room, we invited the television into the dining area. The one remaining setting in homes where people were most likely to communicate, sitting next to and opposite each other around a table, soon shared the fate of the family room. All eyes focus now on the increasingly dominating box, instead of on those who share our real world as we break bread each evening.

In many American homes, the dining area is not even used on a regular basis, as family members grab "something to eat" and head for their TVs or computers. Still, we ask why kids and families can't communicate any more. (And to further complicate the problem, a 1994 Gallup poll reported that 58 percent of American children now have TV sets in their bedrooms.)

Add to this the content of television as it has evolved over the years, and problems compound. We've come a long way since *Leave It to Beaver.* We laugh today at Ward Cleaver reading the paper in the evening, still dressed in his jacket and tie, and June Cleaver vacuuming the carpet in her pumps and pearls; but what did we learn about family values and interpersonal relationships from *Leave It to Beaver* . . . (or, for a later generation, from *Little House on the Prairie,* and still later, *The Cosby Show*) and what do we learn today from *The Simpsons, Beavis and Butthead, Mighty Morphin Power Rangers,* and *Married . . . with Children?*

Michael, What Did You Learn From *Leave It to Beaver?*

"As silly as the show was, as contrived as some of the problems may have been, as little as my family had in common with the Cleavers, I identified with them. I grew up in a home that was distinctly unlike the Cleavers, in a large city that had few of the suburban Norman Rockwellesqe images of the Cleavers' town, and in a family that included four times as many children.

"My non–Anglo-Saxon, and non-affluent family was still very close to its immigrant roots. In spite of all this, my dad was Ward, my mom—whom I can't ever remember *seeing* in pumps and pearls, much less vacuuming the carpet in them—was June, I was Wally, and one of my several younger brothers was The Beave.

"And what did I learn watching that show? I learned how siblings were supposed to talk to one another. I learned how spouses were supposed to talk to one another. I learned about the respect that children showed their parents . . . and the respect that parents showed their children. I learned there were good guys and there were not-so-good guys (remember Eddie Haskell?). I learned that the not-so-good guys were not to be hated, but to be encouraged to do better.

"I learned that there were unpopular kids in the world (remember Lumpy?) that I was called upon not to criticize but, again, to understand. I learned, in short, positive life lessons, which I am happy to say were also taught, more often than not, in school, in church, and in my home.

"I grew up seeing TV as an extension and reflection of my value system, as a reinforcement of what I learned in school, church, and home. Today, what child or parent can honestly say the same thing?"

Zig Ziglar, the motivational speaker and writer who popularized the power of positive thinking for several generations of Americans, has a trademark saying that is very appropriate here: "You are what you are because of what you put into your head; if you want to change what you are, you need to change what you put into your head." We might well ask what is being put into our children's heads. It's not a pleasant thought.

How do we compensate for all this, short of throwing out the TV? Although some families have taken this step (and might be applauded for it), most of us are not prepared to do so. How then do we compensate for the possible impact on the development of interpersonal skills and values of children?

Step one is recognizing the problem: TV does in fact present major challenges as we strive to provide emotional stability in the home. Step two is understanding what problems TV presents, why they are problems, and what steps might be necessary to overcome or compensate for those problems. Step three is to be proactive in taking steps to deal with the issues television creates for your family, be they formal family meetings, restricted TV time, scheduled one-on-one attention, and/or TV-free dinner. The important thing is to address the problem and gain control of the television so that it does not control us. Quite a challenge, but one worth taking.

Physical Signs of Affection

A father shared this experience: "At the close of a long day some years back during which I was successfully ignoring my family, living instead almost entirely within my emotional cave, my son, about twelve at the time, approached me. With the simplicity found only in youth, he said, 'Dad, you haven't hardly even touched me all day!'

"He was right. My silence he could handle. My characteristic introspection was something he had learned was just part of the way old Dad is. However, the fact that not once during the day had I hugged him, patted his shoulder, or even punched him playfully in the arm was more than he could handle. 'You haven't hardly even touched me all day.' What a powerful indictment!"

Communication, experts tell us, is only about 20 percent verbal. The remaining 80 percent is body language, intonation, context, setting, attitude, and so on. The raised eyebrow, the folded arms, the blank stare, the tone of voice, and physical position in relation to the listener all affect the message that is received. However, nothing is more important and powerful than physical touch.

It is unfortunate today that physical touch has become such a sensitive issue because of abuse problems. Teachers are routinely instructed by administrators to avoid touching a student lest that touch be misconstrued, resulting in embarrassment, discomfort, confrontation, lawsuits, or worse. Some parents have also taken this approach and applied it to their families, avoiding physical signs of affection lest their children grow up unwary of its abuses.

Concern about this is, of course, justified; we do not need to be reminded that abuses do occur and must be guarded against. But, when vigilance in preventing abuse leads us to argue for no physical touch at all, we may be contributing to another form of abuse, the abuse of emotional detachment.

Many studies report the critical need for physical touch in newborns. Picking children up, holding them close, and stroking their faces can be critical to their very survival. People who work in nursing homes report that physical touch can make a difference in the quality of life of the elderly, even prolonging their lives. Men and women throughout the world regularly shake hands, embrace, or kiss each other in their daily greeting. Touch can heal, affirm, encourage, validate, and nurture . . . or offend, alienate, and embarrass . . . depending on circumstances. Touch has extraordinary power within the context of families and emotional stability.

Emotional stability in the home is strengthened when family members spontaneously touch each other in affection and care. In addition to making contact, providing closeness, and showing affection, loving physical touch helps children understand the difference between touch that is appropriate and that which isn't.

Couples can model appropriate physical touch by their own natural expressions of it with each other, as well as to their children. Children will have plenty of opportunities from television and the movies to learn how hugs and kisses can be abused; they need to learn from us those natural signs of affection that happy, healthy, emotionally secure people can express without fear.

One final note on the issue of physical touch: We do not believe that corporal punishment is helpful in a family striving for emotional stability. There appears to be little or nothing that corporal punishment teaches other than power, force, violence, pain, and avoidance. What logical connection is there between spanking and teaching? Indeed, it may be an abdication of the parental responsibility to teach through example.

It is truly unfortunate that, as reported by a Gallup poll in December 1995, about half of American parents believe it is "sometimes necessary to punish a child with a good, hard spanking." This is sad commentary on the state of parenting and parent education, and it presents a challenge for all who seek respectful, dignified ways of guiding children. Emotionally stable families ensure that physical contact with children is loving, soothing, comforting, and affirming—not a source of pain.

> ## School-Smart Parenting Tip:
> Avoid spanking and all other negative
> forms of physical contact; teach children
> that imposing physical pain is not an acceptable
> way to get others to do as we wish.

Michael, Carol, and Jennifer

When our daughter, Jennifer, was in her second year of high school, we found ourselves caught in a rescuing situation that we had not anticipated and that, consequently, developed into a major problem. Jennifer, who attends a high school some twenty miles from home, rides a school bus; but the nearest bus stop is some five miles away.

Since the bus stop is nearer to Carol's place of work than to mine, it had fallen to her to drive Jennifer to the school bus stop each morning. As a result, Carol also found herself assuming the job of waking Jennifer up on time to drive with her to the bus stop. Since Jennifer had no options for getting to school other than riding with Mom to the bus stop, Mom felt that it was her duty to go into Jennifer's room numerous times each morning to rouse her from bed and drag her, if necessary, to the car.

What were the consequences if Jennifer refused to get up and get dressed on time? The natural consequence was that she wouldn't get to school that day. Since that was unacceptable to us, we had tried to establish "logical consequences." For failing to accept the responsibility of getting to school each day during the week, she would lose the privilege of going out on the weekend. We discussed this "consequence" with Jennifer. It was in place and it was clear.

It just wasn't working. Mom's day (and, more often than not, Jennifer's day) was ruined by the battle that took place each morning to get Jennifer out of bed. In frustration, Mom let it all out one evening. "Why do I have to deal with this every morning? How come you don't have to battle with your daughter (*your* daughter!) and ruin every day? Why isn't all this business about natural and logical consequences working, Mr. Parenting Expert?"

With all the sensitivity a man typically shows to a woman's emotional state, I jumped immediately into a problem-solving mode (exactly what Carol did *not* want right then). I embarked on an explanation of the distinction between natural and logical consequences, why they are effective in most situations, and how Carol was creating her own problem by not allowing consequences to be effective in this situation.

About a week later, after the dust had settled, we were able to calmly and intelligently discuss Jennifer's morning problems. What we came to realize, after much discussion and debate, was that we were not in fact allowing the consequences to take place. By going into the room six, eight, ten times to ensure that Jennifer was getting up, we were stepping in and preventing her from experiencing the consequences of her actions. In short, we were rescuing her.

Why were we doing this? Why would we step in every day and rescue Jennifer from experiencing what would happen if she failed to take responsibility for getting herself up, something a fifteen-year-old could certainly do by herself? Why were we preventing her from growing in maturity through the experience of real-life lessons? Why? Because it hurt us too much to see her miss school and, possibly, miss a big dance, party, or evening with friends on the weekend.

The dialogue between Mom and Dad was revealing.

"Why do you go in there so often every morning?" I asked.

"Because she won't get up on her own."

"But why can't we just let her experience the consequences of missing school and weekend activities?"

"Because this weekend is her school's homecoming dance, and next weekend is her friend's sixteenth birthday party, and the weekend after that they are all going to Six Flags together, and the weekend after that . . ."

"Well, then," I responded, with characteristic sensitivity, "unless you plan to spend the rest of your life waking up Jennifer in the morning, you'd better learn to accept the unpleasantness of a missed weekend."

So we sat down with Jennifer and frankly and honestly explained the problem from our perspective. We talked about the consequences that were already in place. We checked out with her whether or not she was willing to accept those consequences (she was).

She went out and purchased a backup battery-operated alarm to go with her electric radio alarm. We agreed that, starting with the coming week, we would go into her room just twice to help her get up (this is called "weaning"; rather than go "cold turkey" with her, we limited our involvement to twice each morning, then a few months later to once, and finally to not at all). We then discussed her plans for the next weekend (it was the weekend of her friend's sixteenth birthday party), and made a contract.

Monday came and Jennifer was awake and eating breakfast even before we had awakened. On Tuesday, she was still asleep when we awoke, and when her alarms went off she remained in bed. But on the second visit from Mom she was up and ready. Then came Wednesday, which turned out to be The Day of Reckoning.

Mom and I got up at our regular times. Jennifer's radio alarm went off as it always did, followed five minutes later by her battery-operated alarm. Both the radio was playing (too loud, of course) and the alarm was buzzing, but Jennifer remained under the covers. Mom went in the first time, shook her gently, got the usual muffled response, and left. Ten minutes later, she repeated the procedure, getting the same response. On Tuesday, that had resulted in Jennifer's joining us at the breakfast table. But today, no one was emerging from her room.

The minutes ticked away with only a half-hour remaining before Mom would have to leave, and still no Jennifer. Should I check inside just one more time? she wondered. My body language said no.

Twenty minutes before Mom would have to leave, there was still no Jennifer. "Maybe I didn't shake her hard enough the second time," Mom suggested.

"Let her be," was my reply.

Ten minutes before time to leave, and no Jennifer. Mom protested: "But Saturday is the big sixteenth birthday party. I can't just let her miss it!"

I answered, "Nobody wants her to miss that party, but we need to let the consequences take place. Let her be!" (It's so easy to be firm when the *other* parent will end up receiving the brunt of the child's wrath!) So we both left for work, leaving Jennifer behind, allowing her to wake up some time later to realize what had happened and deal with it on her own throughout the day.

When we got home that evening, we resisted the temptation to dump on Jennifer . . . "Look what happened! How can you be so irresponsible! How many times did we tell you to get up as soon as your alarm goes off! When will you ever grow up?!?" Instead, we allowed her to share her own disappointment with us.

When she asked, as was inevitable, whether this really meant that she had to miss the party, we simply reminded her what the arrangement was that we had all agreed to, and we left it at that. She asked us two or three more times the next few days, and we gave the same answer. But there were no tantrums about the missed party.

When Saturday night came and we had no plans of our own to go anywhere, we rented a video, and the three of us—Mom, Dad, and Jennifer—stayed home and enjoyed each other's company. Did Jennifer miss the party? Very much so. Did it hurt us? Again, very much so. However it's been several years now, and she has never failed to get up on time for school since. We are confident that she learned from the experience, and years from now, when she is out there in the "real world," we are confident that her employers will always be able to count on her to get to work every day and on time.

What made it work was that we used consequences rather than punishment. Jennifer was not punished for failing to get up on time for school; instead, she was allowed to experience the results of her actions. What's the difference? The difference lies in how we approach the situation, and how, as a result of our approach, the child perceives her role in what happens. We applied the principles discussed in chapter 9, "Developing Strong Systemic Skills," to help her develop the skills she needed in order to be responsible for herself.

In working with Jennifer regarding her getting up on time for school, we had both natural and logical consequences working. The natural consequences of not getting up on time were simply that she missed school and would most likely fall behind in her work.

An argument could be made that missing school was enough of a consequence and there should be no need for establishing logical consequences in this situation. However, school was a much lower priority for Jennifer at that time than it was for us, and we feared (with good reason!) that she would be willing to miss a day every now and then if the only consequence was falling behind in her work.

So we sat down with Jennifer and decided upon logical consequences, agreeing that the privilege of going out with friends over the weekend would be dependent upon her accepting and fulfilling the responsibility of going to school. Is this related? We think so. Note the connection between privileges and responsibilities.

Is it reasonable? Again, we think so. If she misses school during the week, she loses the privilege of going out for just that weekend, not for the whole month. (It is the *inevitability* of the consequence, not its *severity*, that matters most here; in fact, severity is frequently counter-productive as it tends to lead to rebellion.) Was it handled respectfully, both beforehand and after? We did our best to ensure that it was.

Again, the opposite of a consequential approach is punishment. And the difference is not in *what* happens so much as it is in *how* the child perceives the whole experience. We could have simply punished Jennifer for not getting up on time. We could have had no discussion about the problem. We could have simply declared that she was grounded for the weekend . . . or for the month . . . or "forever." We could have worked hard to make sure that during her grounding she "suffered," rather than have the opportunity for a fun evening watching a video with her parents. We could have dumped adultism upon adultism on top of her. We could have shamed, blamed, and criticized her for not being responsible.

Had we done so, what might her perception of the experience have been? What would she have learned from it? Would she have learned that when she makes certain choices in life, those choices carry with them, of necessity, certain specific consequences? Or would she have learned that life consists of other people doing things to you?

Therein lies the difference between a consequential approach and a punishment approach to working with children. In the former, my choices determine what happens to me; in the latter, what happens is what other people do to me.

Striving for a home environment in which consequences are the rule and punishments are the exception will help provide the emotional stability that results from the perception that the outcomes I experience result from choices that I make. And there is no better road to responsibility than that.

Consequences vs. Rewards and Punishments

Interestingly, all that has been said above regarding consequences vs. punishments applies just as well to consequences vs. rewards, although the hazards of a rewards-based environment may not be as obvious as those of a punishment-based environment. For a fascinating look at the dangers implicit in rewards-based systems, see Alfie Kohn's provocative study, *Punished by Rewards*.

For now, suffice it to say that rewards can serve as just another way to control others ("Do what I want you to do, and I will give you this."), they tend to be disruptive of relationships because they focus on winners and losers, they ignore the root causes of problems, and they discourage risk-taking and creativity. Indeed, a good argument could be made that rewards can be even worse than punishments, because rewards take a positive thing and ruin it, whereas punishment only takes a negative thing and makes it worse.

To the degree to which we can teach through natural consequences and results rather than rewards when working with our children, they will learn to appreciate their achievements as valuable in and of themselves, rather than because of a reward they get.

If we give our child $5 for getting an "A" on her report card, we are communicating to her that the reason for getting the "A" is the $5. We are much more effective as parents when we sit down with her and ask her what she thinks helped her to get such a good grade, what she learned from the experiences that led up to the "A," and how she can use that information to continue to be successful in that area and other areas of her life. In this way we encourage intrinsic motivation that will help her look at opportunities as chances to grow. This also demonstrates our interest in her real achievements, something that is worth much more than $5.

> **School-Smart Parenting Tip:**
> **Discuss consequences and results, rather than using rewards and punishments; this will teach that what happens is largely a result of what we do, rather than what those we love do to us.**

Leaving School Issues at School and Home Issues at Home

Now for the last word on rewards, punishments, and consequences: Let teachers deal with school issues and parents with home issues.

If children get in trouble at school and receive some consequence for it (time out, missed recess, detention), there is no need to complicate the matter by adding consequences at home. We have seen too many examples of home/school communication breaking down because children fail to tell their parents about school problems out of fear that they will be punished at home.

When we are apprised of school problems, all we need to do is verbally demonstrate our interest in, and support for, the school's concern. It is always helpful to sit down with children and ask what happened, what they believe contributed to the problem, and what they plan to do to resolve the problem and avoid it in the future.

That's all. The school should not try to deal with issues that come up at home, and parents should not try to apply discipline for at-school infractions. What is needed is mutual support and the willingness to work with children to help identify what they can do to resolve the issue.

If we handle school discipline problems that way we increase the possibility that our children will communicate with us about them. Otherwise, they will work diligently to keep those problems from us, even to the extent of destroying teacher notes, changing report card grades, and lying. Support and encouragement yield open communication; criticism and punishment yield avoidance and rebellion. The choice is clear.

> ### School-Smart Parenting Tip:
> **Leave school problems at school and home problems at home. If your child gets in trouble at school, work with him or her to identify what happened, why it happened, and what can be done next time to avoid it; but don't add your own discipline to school discipline.**

"Because I Said So!"

How many times have you found yourself using expressions that your parents used on you, and you swore you'd never use on your own children? We all do it—not because we want to, but because we haven't taken the time to identify alternatives to those tired, old sayings.

Rather than reflect on what we would really like to say, we replay the old scripts that are deep within our memory bank. We want to be more affirming (at least more creative!), but we do not stop to think about just how.

Well, let's think about it now. Let's take a look at some of those dreaded expressions and come up with alternatives. And let's shock our kids the next time we have an unpleasant encounter with them by using a new expression, a firm yet respectful expression that will enable them to focus on the problem at hand, rather than get distracted by our sarcasm. The following chart (**Alternatives to Routine Expressions**), shows examples taken from a very informal survey of students ages six through fourteen that was conducted at a certain Dallas-area elementary school with which Michael has some association:

ALTERNATIVES TO ROUTINE EXPRESSIONS

The Old Script	The New and Improved Script
"Because I said so." —suggests that the reason you should do certain things rather than other things is simply my arbitrary decision.	"Because it's the right thing to do." —suggests that you should do certain things rather than other things because of the intrinsic worthiness or correctness of those things.
"No one ever said life is fair."—discounts the child's feelings and communicates the perception that life is	"I can understand how you might feel that way. And I share your wish that life would be fair. Now how can we make the best of this

just that way and there's nothing you can do about it.

"What part of 'NO' don't you understand?"—okay, maybe this was cute the first dozen or so times we said it, but it's old now and its only value is as sarcasm, which has no value at all. Sarcasm only teaches children to be sarcastic; it doesn't teach respectfulness.

"If everyone jumped off the cliff, would you do likewise?" —besides having no relevance whatsoever to the issue at stake, this expression prevents us from accepting the opportunity of communicating our family values.

situation?" —affirms the child's feelings and communicates that we can still influence outcomes even if life isn't fair.

"The reason I am saying 'no' is because this matter is very important to me. Later, when you are ready to discuss this respectfully, I will do my best to explain it to you." —communicates that there are some matters in life that the parent must assume responsibility for, whether or not the child likes it, but does so respectfully and communicates a willingness to explain the reason.

"I can understand your wanting to go, particularly if some of your friends are going. But as we discussed yesterday at our family meeting, we do not go to those movies because we believe they communicate values that we find very disrespectful." —this addresses the specific issue directly and respectfully and communicates the reason for the decision, while at

(continued)

(Alternatives to Routine Expressions—continued)

The Old Script	The New and Improved Script
	the same time reaffirming the family's values.
"When I was your age . . ."—when used to tell a story in a friendly setting, this can be a very effective way to share our pasts with our children, and they will listen with anticipation; if it is used to show our children how tough we are or how smart we are or how much better they have it now (and why don't they appreciate that?), it only serves to miss the opportunity to share our past in a way that allows them to enjoy the experience.	"I can remember when I was young, we used to . . ." —since we have by and large lost the opportunity to use "when I was your age . . ." without causing a rolling of the eyes, it's probably best to try a different opener; the important point is that we should - avoid trying to communi cate out superiority ("When I was in school, we had to memorize *The Midnight Ride of Paul Revere,* not just know who wrote it!") when telling stories about our past if we want our children to listen to them, learn from them and be willing to share more with us.

As you might imagine, the students had a lot of fun identifying their most hated expressions. There were more (a lot more!), but those noted above constitute the top five. One very interesting comment by a younger student was quite enlightening: "Mom's voice changes when she talks about me in public; it's all squeaky and babylike." Why do we do that? Why do we treat our developing young people as if their development were arrested at the infancy stage? Why don't we just talk to them and about them the same way we speak to and about adults? What communication skills—infantile or adult-like—do we want to model for our children?

Two themes were common to the expressions that the students identified: sarcasm and authoritarianism. Sarcastic expressions ("Are you waiting for a personal invitation?" "I hope you have a kid just like you!") led the list, followed closely by authoritarian ones ("Because I'm your mother." "I'm the parent; you're the child."). Our challenge as parents is to avoid sarcasm and authoritarianism by modeling firmness, with dignity and respect.

"Firmness" communicates what needs to be done *authoritatively*, which, contrary to the word "authoritarian," suggests a higher authority or reason or principle, to which we *all* are subject, Mom and Dad as well as the children. "With dignity and respect" reminds us that our children do not occupy some lower level of the species than we do, and they really do deserve to be treated respectfully, just as we ourselves deserve to be treated.

We can change the words we use by making the conscious effort to identify the words that do damage, actively substituting more respectful words, and putting them into practice. We will feel better about it, and our children will feel better about it. They will also reap the benefit of having learned positive and affirming expressions to use in their interactions with their own children when they become parents. Not a bad gift to give them!

Looking for Solutions: Problem-Solving with Empathy

Parents most frequently get careless with the words they use with children when criticizing them for something they have done wrong. This often reflects a knee-jerk reaction based on assigning blame, rather than focusing on a solution to the problem.

Therefore, a good first step in improving verbal responses to problems with children is to make the perceptual shift from focusing on blame to focusing on solutions. Changing our approach when dealing with homework problems, for example, from "How many times do I have to tell you to get your homework done before bedtime?" to "It appears that our previous plan about getting all your homework done before bedtime isn't working, so what will it take to get it done?" sets the stage for an approach in which the child is involved in finding a solution to his or her problem.

Recognizing a problem as needing a solution, rather than just needing blame, and doing so respectfully, creates a positive environment in which to work through the problem. A problem-solving process can be broken down into various components in a number of ways. The following six-step approach is particularly helpful when working with children.

1. **Ask** the child what she sees as the problem and what things are contributing to it. Listen carefully in an effort to understand the child's perceptions and get into her world. In checking her perceptions, avoid as much as possible the "why" word, which tends to come across as interrogatory and accusatory, often resulting in an "I don't know." Use "What would be some reasons that you think you're having problems with this?" rather than "Why are you having problems with this?"

2. **Reflect** back to the child your understanding of what has been said, checking with her to make sure that you've got it right: "Let me be sure I understand what you're saying here. You're saying that you think you're having trouble getting your homework done before bed-

time because you put off starting it until it's too late. You don't like starting it as soon as you get home and then you keep putting it off. So, the more you put it off, the bigger the job seems to get. Is that right?"

3. **Show empathy** for the problem: "I can understand that. I usually like a break too right after I get home from work . . . before I jump into any chores at home. As a matter of fact, I can remember when I was in school and homework was the last thing I wanted to do as soon as I got home."

4. **Check** the child's ideas. "What ideas do you have for dealing with this issue?" Often, if we have handled the discussion respectfully and have demonstrated real interest in the child's thoughts on the issue, she will be able to come up with solutions on her own.

5. **Explore** solutions. If necessary, share your own thoughts on the problem, but continue to involve the child in the solution: "What do you think would happen if you took a short break right after you got home and then did just one part of your homework, took another break and then did another part until it was done? (allow a response) Sometimes when we break a large task into smaller parts and spread them out, it's easier to get it all done. How do you think that might work?" Notice that we've avoided lecturing, offering our suggestion in the form of a question: "What do you think would happen if . . ."

6. **Agree** on a solution, either one that your child mentioned, one that you mentioned, or some combination of the two. "What will you need to do to make that happen?" "What would you like me to do to support you?" Agree to check back in a week or two to see how the plan is working.

When we shift from blaming to problem solving, we take the pressure off children and encourage them to take ownership of their problems. We offer wisdom and

School-Smart Parenting Tip:

**Approach misbehavior as a problem
to be solved rather than as an excuse
for shaming and blaming.**

experience as a resource, but we keep children focused on finding solutions.

Criticizing, on the other hand, lets the child off the hook. The homework problem becomes the parent's, not the child's. His only problem is waiting out the verbal barrage. Once the shaming and blaming is over, the child is home free. The parent is left with the frustration . . . and an unresolved problem for which he or she will continue to be responsible for bringing up again and again.

The decision is clear. If you want to be responsible for the problem, then shame, blame, and criticize the child. If you want the child to be responsible for solving the problem, engage in problem solving with empathy.

Keep Your Mouth Shut and Act

One of our favorite cartoons from *The Far Side* shows a man lecturing to his dog: "How many times do I have to tell you, Rover, that you're not supposed to scratch the furniture. I just bought this furniture last week! It isn't even paid for yet, and now it has these scratches all over it! Do I have to leave you outside all day? Do I have to return you to the pound? What do I have to do to get you to behave?" And what the dog is hearing is this: "Blah, blah, blah, blah, Rover, blah, blah, blah, blah, blah . . ."

Think of that cartoon whenever you find yourself lecturing to children. The more we lecture, the more we sound like the man in the cartoon. And, like Rover, our children are hearing . . . "Blah, blah, blah, blah, blah, blah, blah . . ."

When working with children, less is often best. The more we say, the more they tune us out. The fewer words we use, the more they hear what we are saying. State concerns—firmly, respectfully, and briefly; then, be quiet and act with dignity.

Take Care of Your Own Needs

Next time you fly, consider the words of flight attendants as they explain how to use the oxygen masks: "If you are flying with a small child, apply your own oxygen mask to yourself first, then help your child put his or her mask on!" The implication is clear: You will be of little help to your child if you do not first ensure that you are taken care of. Once you are safe, you can give your full attention to the needs of the child.

This is a perfect metaphor for the importance of parents ensuring that their own needs are met before they can effectively provide emotional stability for children. When we are drained of energy, have had no time all day for ourselves, or feel unloved, we need to attend to these needs first in order to be effective in meeting children's needs.

Often, what stands in the way of taking care of oneself is guilt. Guilt is that little voice within that tells us that what we are doing is not quite right. Healthy guilt has value, and we have all encountered people who could use a little bit more of it. However, guilt is frequently unnecessary and unhealthy. Sometimes we feel guilty when we are not rushing to school to bail children out of the little problems they have gotten themselves into. We feel guilty if we are not attending to their every need. We feel guilty if we are not entertaining them, reading to them, or playing with them. We feel guilt and feel guilt . . . until we are drained of energy and love. This robs us of energy to deal with children effectively and leaves us with nothing to fall back on but the very knee-jerk reactions we have been working so hard to overcome—blaming, shaming, directing, criticizing, scolding, and yelling.

To avoid this, we need to accept the fact that our own needs are important and legitimate. We need to do something for ourselves—go off alone with a good book, call a friend to go out for lunch, take a warm bath, go shopping. We need to announce this, without apology, to our families. Only in this way can we experience the renewal that allows us to be at our best—for ourselves and those we love.

A Place Where You Want to Be

Through family dinners, family meetings, and family nights; physical signs of affection; alternatives to TV; logical consequences rather than punishment; respectful rather than critical language; problem solving rather than blaming; and self-renewal, what we seek is the emotional security of a home environment in which adults and children feel welcome and comfortable. Is home a place where children want to be? When choices arise between staying home with the family and engaging in unhealthy activities, will they choose to stay home? Are they comfortable inviting their friends over?

Starting early to make sure that home is a comfortable place to be; a place of encouragement, support, and affirmation; a place where each person is loved unconditionally; and a place free from constant nagging and criticism will increase the probability that we can answer these questions affirmatively.

All You Need Is Love

The family characterized by emotional stability is the family in which love is given unconditionally, not in response to anything the child (or spouse) does or does not do. When we tell children that we love them for the grades they got or for the work they did around the house or for the gift they just gave us, we communicate that love is something given in return for something else. True love is given freely, unconditionally, and because of who you are, not because of what you do.

Consider the beauty of this principle in this story of a little girl, Jessica, who lives with her grandmother. It is Grandma's birthday, and little Jessica has nothing to give her, but on the way home from school she spots some dandelions in a field and picks a bunch. She sneaks them into the house when her grandmother isn't looking, finds an old vase, fills it with water, arranges the dandelions as best she can, and, beaming, presents them: "Grandma, I picked these flowers for you. Happy birthday!"

Grandma, not anticipating the gift and seeing a vase filled with weeds rather than Jessica's present, exclaims: "Well, thank you, Jessica, but these aren't flowers; these are weeds."

And little Jessica replies: "If you love them enough, Grandma, they are no longer weeds."

Sometimes it all comes down to that simple truth: If you love them enough, they are no longer weeds. Little Jessica knows, in the simple wisdom of a child, that since unconditional love can move mountains, it can certainly turn weeds into flowers.

A family characterized by emotional stability is a family where love can turn weeds into flowers. Family members experience the security of knowing that, whatever they face in the outside world, when they walk through the doors of their home, they are accepted, affirmed, and loved.

School-Smart Parenting Tip:
Love children unconditionally; help them
feel secure that your love is for them,
regardless of what they do or achieve.

Children raised in such a home can go freely and confidently into that outside world, including school, knowing that they are loved and lovable, fully open to all the world can offer. They enter the world of school seeking opportunities to fully maximize their potential. They travel through it without unnecessary baggage to weigh them down. They go through life knowing that when they encounter adversity, they have that secure, safe place called home to which they can always return. This is the greatest asset we can provide for them.

Chapter 15

Walking the Talk— Modeling

Example is not the main thing in influencing others. It is the only thing.

—Albert Schweitzer

One of the most powerful teaching strategies is that of "walking the talk!" A key to this asset lies in recognizing that we cannot change other people, not even our children. We can only change ourselves. However, in doing so, we offer a model for others to emulate.

Basketball superstar Charles Barkley of the Houston Rockets and the Olympics "Dream Team" responded to critics of his lifestyle by saying that he did " . . . not consider it his responsibility to be a role model, . . . [his] responsibility was to be a professional basketball player and win games"; and it was "the parents' responsibility to be their children's role models." He was right . . . and he was wrong!

He was wrong because every man and woman on earth has the potential to be a role model. The more visible we are in the public eye, the greater that responsibility is. For sports figures, who occupy a position near reverence for young people, the responsibility to be a role model grows in proportion to their fame. He was right, however, when he correctly identified the responsibility of the parent to "walk the talk" if we want children to listen to our words. In other words, the old adultism, "Do what I say, not what I do," doesn't work.

Actually, it does work, if we want our children to grow up telling their children to "do what I say, not what I do." Highlight it, underline it, write it on a file card and tape it to your mirror. There is no more effective way to teach than through "walking the talk," or what we more familiarly refer to as modeling.

Most people have heard the three most important things to know about real estate: location, location, location. Without too much exaggeration, it could be said that the three most important things to know about parenting are: modeling, modeling, modeling. Modeling is little more than deciding to look at what we need to do, rather than to what children need to do, then following through. "Action speaks louder than words!"

> **School-Smart Parenting Tip:**
> **Walk the talk! Model the behaviors**
> **you want your children to learn.**

Here are twelve specific ways that parents can model effective behaviors that support children during their school years. Some of these are reaffirmations of points made in previous chapters, with the emphasis now placed on active modeling.

Others are additional challenges for reflection and consideration. In all cases, the emphasis is placed on the importance of "walking the talk" so that children can observe the integration of actions and values.

1. Respect time commitments

Have you ever been frustrated by the spouse, friend, or employee who is seldom on time? Have you found their excuses—"Oh, I'm just late for everything; that's just the way I am!"—somewhat less than satisfying? Do you struggle with a negative mindset that justifies continual tardiness in yourself or in children?

If so, it's helpful to realize that being on time is nothing more than a habit, and habits can be changed. If we wish to change the habit of tardiness in children, or prevent the habit from forming, the first step is to model punctuality ourselves. When we are on time for our many commitments—soccer practice, ballet class, movies, place of worship, school—we model the importance of respecting the needs of others. We model self-discipline and responsibility. We also model respect for commitments. In doing so, we encourage children to develop the habit of punctuality, which will be deeply appreciated by their friends and business associates for the rest of their lives.

When we drop our children off late for school, we are communicating: "School is not really that important. Rules are made to be ignored. Commitments to teachers and classmates are not really that critical." We demonstrate that being a member of a group does not involve being responsible to that group. We also suggest that the child is really not that important to the success of the group.

School-Smart Parenting Tip:
Be on time! Teach your children by
example that time commitments
are responsibilities not just to
themselves, but to others.

A child raised with disregard for time commitments is very much in danger of developing negative attitudes toward societal rules, the expectations of employees, and the needs of others. The best way to teach children to be on time is to model that behavior ourselves.

2. Read . . . to yourself and to your children

When we read, we model the importance of reading. Let children see you read. Let them experience your modeling the behavior of turning off the television, sitting down in the family room, and spending some quality time reading.

In addition to modeling the importance of reading, we also model the value of quiet time, reflection, and studying. J.R.R. Tolkien set the stage for the wondrous fantasy world he created very early in *The Hobbit,* his introduction to *The Lord of the Rings* trilogy, by noting that it all takes place "in the quiet of the world, when there was less noise and more green."

We've come a long way from that world of quiet and tranquility, but books are one of the best ways to bring us back to it. By reading ourselves, we model that peacefulness and quiet solitude are essential ingredients of emotional stability.

Read to your children. Start reading to children as soon as you start speaking to them. Read as long as you can hold their attention. Read at levels above their own reading ability level. (First-graders, for example, can probably understand third- and fourth-grade-level books being read to them, even though they may be unable to read them for understanding themselves.)

Reading to children accomplishes several things. Certainly, children's reading skills are reinforced. They can follow the words with their eyes, say the words to themselves, and read along out loud with us. If we resist the temptation to create a formal teaching situation (a behavior guaranteed to reduce our children's interest in sitting down with us the next time we try to read to them), the experience can reinforce their developing reading skills.

More importantly, reading to a child offers a very special opportunity to provide one-on-one attention. Such attention says: "You are significant in my eyes; you are worthy of my time; you deserve this special moment with me."

This one-on-one attention, combined with the physical closeness, touch, and warmth that exists in the parent/child reading environment, is powerful medicine—both preventive and curative—for much of what can ail children. There are even potential medical benefits of personal attention. The positive effects of a soothing voice and physical touch have been understood for centuries and are being rediscovered today, even in our medication-biased world.

Take the opportunity to read to your children. Let them have your undivided attention. Let them hear your voice. Let them feel your warmth next to them. They will tend to be more physically and emotionally healthy because of it. Also, their interest in reading will generally improve!

3. Be discriminating in your TV viewing

Is television the place we want children to find role models? TV is a wonderful invention, offering entertainment, culture, news, and education to millions who otherwise would never have the opportunity. However, as welcome as these benefits are, there are negatives, and we have become increasingly aware of them in recent years.

Just complaining about the values kids gain from TV is not an effective approach. Unless, of course, we want to raise children who address their own problems by complaining about them. Modeling discriminate use of TV is a much more effective approach.

Some years ago, the late University of Toronto English professor Marshall McLuhan taught that "the medium is the message." McLuhan's contention that "the medium itself carries its own message, regardless of the content of the medium" is recognized today as one of the more profound insights of the twentieth-century communications revolution.

Nowhere does the message of the medium have such a powerful impact on our lives than in television. The rapidly changing, multi-patterned, hyperactive images of television, whether they project the alphabet on *Sesame Street* or a screeching car and blasting bullets on any number of crime shows, have affected everything in our society. From education (television is implicated in the proliferation of Attention Deficit Disorder and Hyperactive Disorder diagnoses) to politics (the art of the sound bite provides advantages to the telegenic candidate), the effects of television are significant.

A parental challenge is to model the effective use of television, to take advantage of TV's ability to bring news, culture, entertainment, and even insight. We also need to control television and monitor its use. In short, we need to take advantage of T.V.'s positive opportunities, while remaining conscious of its potential problems.

Keeping the TV off unless we want to see something specific is helpful. Ensuring that the TV does not dominate our households is critical. In a home where the TV is on continuously, what lessons are being taught? Primarily, we teach children that the television is the ultimate authority in their lives. We communicate that this box, which occupies a place of honor in the family room and is constantly talking to us with words and pictures, is the source for everything important in life.

Go into a child's room and you will immediately learn what is most important to him or her by what occupies a place of honor and grabs your attention. Maybe it's sports, maybe rock stars, maybe boyfriends or girlfriends, maybe cars. Whatever is important to the child will be evident immediately—on the walls, bookshelves, bulletin boards, and mirrors. The same applies to the home with the continuously running television. That home screams out to all who enter: This machine is the most important thing in this house; whatever may concern you at the moment, whatever you may wish to communicate, whatever need you may have, all is secondary to the news, sports, sitcoms, and talk shows that this machine is featuring.

Are we too dramatic? We don't think so! Does anyone doubt that TV is one of the most effective teaching tools that currently exists? If this is so, by allowing the television to run continuously, we allow it to assume the role of children's primary teacher. Therefore television is teaching them what is really important, what values we should hold, how we are to treat each other, how we are to talk to each other, how we are to spend money, what beer will make us young and beautiful and popular. If television were not such a powerful teacher, would companies continue to spend billions yearly to advertise their products through that medium?

TV can in fact replace Mom, Dad, Grandma, Granddad, aunts, uncles, community leaders, and all other possible sources of advice, wisdom, and nurturing for young children. Therefore, the issue of television requires our proactive response. There are shows that promote positive values, and VCRs make it possible to proactively look for videos with messages that support our own value systems. The choice is really ours: Do we model discriminating use of the TV by turning it on for a positive program or video, then turning it back off when it's over, or do we allow TV itself to be the model by keeping it on all day?

School-Smart Parenting Tip:
Apply your family values to the
selection, use, and influence of TV.

---

4. Project a positive attitude about school

A father entered the principal's office, sat down at the conference table, folded his hands sheepishly in his lap, and confessed, "You know, I have to admit that I'm a bit intimidated by being in your office." This man stood six feet, four inches tall and weighed close to three hundred pounds—over a half foot taller than and nearly twice the weight of the principal . . . yet he felt intimidated!

How we approach children's schooling reflects, in large measure, the memories we have from our own schooling. If those memories are positive and empowering, we generally communicate this attitude to children. They, in turn, will most likely approach their own schooling in a positive way. If instead, our memories of school are unpleasant (like the dad who was intimidated by being in the office), we tend to communicate unpleasantness and fearfulness and negativism to children, thereby diminishing their chances for success and happiness in school.

An effective way to project a positive attitude about school is to use words that suggest positive expectations of what children will experience there. Consider the chart on the next page **(Contrasting Expressions),** and ask yourself what perceptions the child might develop from each:

CONTRASTING EXPRESSIONS

Expression	Probable Outcome
1. "Oh, you poor dear! How will you ever stay awake from 8:00 until 3:00? That's too long for a little six-year-old!"	The child will use "I'm too tired" as an excuse for low achievement.

—or—

"Now that you're in the big school, you get to spend the whole day at school. You are getting so big and smart!"	The child will see herself as a growing, developing young person eager to meet new challenges.

2. "Look at all that homework! How do they expect a fourth-grader to do that much	The child will develop the habit of complaining as a response to life's challenges, and will learn to see work?" difficulty not as something to overcome but as an excuse for avoidance of responsibilities.

—or—

"That's an impressive homework assignment! They must think very highly of you to expect that much from you."	The child will see himself as becoming a big boy with bigger responsibilities. He may still not appreciate the increased homework load, but he will see it less as a burden and more as an affirmation of his developing maturity.

(continued)

(Contrasting Expressions—continued)

Expression	Probable Outcome
3. "I was a real cut-up in school. I think I spent more time in the principal's office than in the classroom."	The child will see getting in trouble at school as acceptable behavior.

—or—

Expression	Probable Outcome
"I got in trouble at school a few times too, but I regret it because it hurt me and it hurt the class, and it prevented the teacher from being able to do what she was there to do."	The child will learn that even though he may get in trouble at school from time to time, it is not acceptable because it hurts himself, his classmates, and his teacher. He learns to respect others' needs, not just his own wants.

Many more examples could be given, but these three should suffice to emphasize how the expressions we use affect how children see themselves in relation to their schooling. If your memories of schooling are unpleasant, try hard, first, to identify the cause of that unpleasantness and, second, to consciously avoid communicating that unpleasantness to children. Children will encounter their own unpleasantness, even in the most positive school environments. It is helpful to spare them the burden of our projections.

5. Show active interest in your child's schooling

Homework is your child's responsibility, not yours. However, we can communicate to children, through active interest, that homework is important and relevant. By engaging them in conversation about their homework

> ## School-Smart Parenting Tip:
> **Children are more likely to see school experiences as leading to productive outcomes when parents project hopeful and optimistic attitudes toward school.**

("What kinds of things do you have for homework tonight?" "What are your plans for doing your homework tonight?" "Teach me something that you learned in school today."), we communicate that we are interested in their school lives and support their efforts.

Further, we model the importance of homework when we make a point of doing our own "homework" in their presence. Whatever the nature of our work during the day, we probably have some work that needs attention after regular hours. Teachers certainly do! Doing that work, diligently (if not cheerfully!) in the presence of children further communicates the importance of attention to homework.

We communicate to children that we are really interested in their schooling by getting to know the teachers' names, attending PTA meetings, actively involving ourselves in conferences, and going to class plays and other school activities. Our physical presence communicates to children that they are important enough for us to take time out of our days for them.

Further, we can show real interest by asking questions that invite thoughtful responses. Most parents learn through experience that "Did you have a good day?" rarely invites more than a grunt in response. When we shift to a question such as "What is the most interesting thing that happened in school today?" we help focus children's thought processes on specific events, making a more meaningful response likely.

Other expressions that help our children focus their thoughts, resulting in a greater probability of thoughtful responses, are: "What is one new thing you learned in school today?" "What was one good thing that happened in school today?" and even "What was one thing that didn't work out so well in school today?" (Avoid using the last question in isolation. Try to follow it up with "What was one thing that worked out well in school today?" so the child doesn't stay focused on negatives.)

One reason to ask a child to talk about one thing that didn't work out so well is to communicate to them that we know life isn't always perfect, and we support them in facing challenges. It is important to follow this up with an exploration of something positive in order to maintain a sense of optimism.

Being physically present at school when it is appropriate is helpful in communicating real interest in the schooling part of children's lives. Talking to them and listening to them talk about school experiences reinforces this interest while creating opportunities for them to verbalize thoughts, explore perceptions, and validate their experiences. When we combine this with respect for the privacy regarding school that they need from time to time, we model communication with us as a safe and supportive process.

6. Model problem-solving skills

Looking for solutions rather than blame shifts the focus to the "what" rather than the "who," thereby freeing all involved to stand back and objectively review situations. Looking for solutions rather than blame places no one on the defensive and no one on the offensive. It unites all in a common mission, looking for a solution to the problem.

Among the most effective of numerous ways to model problem-solving processes is the EIAG process emphasized by H. Stephen Glenn and Jane Nelsen in *Raising Self-Reliant Children in a Self-Indulgent World* (Prima). EIAG (pronounced "eye-ag") is an acronym for Experience-Identify-Analyze-Generalize. Simply stated, EIAG is an invitation to see experiences as opportunities for growth rather than as excuses for blaming, criticizing, fault-finding, or discounting. It is a process of focusing on an Experience by Identifying ("What happened?"), Analyzing ("What may have caused it to happen?"), then Generalizing ("How does this influence our response or solution?").

When we sit down with a child, for example after he failed a test, and engage him in dialogue about what happened, what things caused it to happen, and how he can use this knowledge to handle this kind of situation more effectively in the future, we model problem solving. We demonstrate interest in what is going on for the child. We also show respect for his capabilities and a belief in his ability to improve. EIAG is an effective approach, one that avoids lecturing and blaming while actively showing support.

When we have problems to solve, involving children as consultants when appropriate is helpful. At least share your process with them so they can observe and experience problem solving with you. Using such a process as EIAG in family meetings is also helpful as a way of teaching through modeling. While it takes a bit more time to model and involve than to offer the standard lecture, it is definitely more effective in the long run!

7. Teach respect by being respectful

We effectively model respect by showing it in our interaction with people in our lives . . . including children. When Mom is shopping with her daughter, she models respect in how she speaks to the salespeople. When she takes her son to work, she models respect in how she speaks to her associates, particularly those who work under her.

When Dad is at his daughter's soccer game, he models respect in how he speaks to the coaches and referees. Simply put, we model respect continuously through our daily interactions with others. Children learn respect from what they observe and experience with us.

One particular problem regarding respect that we encounter with some frequency should be addressed here: the issue of how spouses treat each other and how that example often translates to children's perceptions of gender.

Children raised in a home in which the most significant member of either gender is treated disrespectfully, with little regard for their opinions, feelings, capabilities, and needs, are likely to universalize this attitude. Their attitude may become significant in how they respond to teachers and others.

As you deal with your spouse, be aware that children learn from your interaction, and may apply this learning in their own lives . . . for good or for ill. Modeling healthy dialogue, collaboration, and affirmation as we deal with each other is, therefore, essential. Make a conscious effort to avoid the "barriers" (which show disrespect) and use the "builders" (which convey respect) from chapter 2, "Barriers and Builders," when you deal with people.

8. Demonstrate respect for those in the teaching profession

In 1995, an article in the *Dallas Morning News* relayed the story of several Dallas Independent School District administrators who, found guilty of minor infractions, were "demoted" to the status of teacher. The clear message was that those in personnel decision-making positions at DISD considered teaching a lower-status position, therefore "demotion" to teaching would be understood as discipline for the infractions. As you might imagine, the school district was hit with a barrage of criticism; not only teachers, but many parents and even school administrators, were offended at this slight to the teaching profession.

Rightly so! A school administrator has decision-making powers that can affect, positively or negatively, the future of children's schooling. However, with the exception of their parents, no people have greater influence on children than their teachers.

Considering their influence, teachers generally are overworked, underpaid, and under-appreciated. This is a national tragedy. When men who spend their lives hitting a piece of cowhide with a stick and running around in a circle to celebrate are paid more in a year than the average teacher will make in a lifetime, we have serious problems with national priorities.

Because we tend to measure not only success but also dignity and worth in terms of income levels, we must be vigilant that children do not perceive teachers as less significant because they are not compensated like other professionals. (The same can be said, by the way, of the overworked, underpaid, and under-appreciated in any number of other helping professions, not to mention numerous service positions, in our society.)

Every job, occupation, and profession is worthy of dignity and respect. The extensive and long-lasting influence of the teacher on the child, however, compels us to reflect on the importance of raising children with a special respect for teachers.

Lee Iacocca, as CEO of Chrysler Motor Company, once said, "In a perfect world, the greatest among us would become teachers . . . and everyone else would have to settle for something less. Because passing our history, traditions, and the keys to civilization on to the next generation ought to be, and is, the greatest honor and responsibility anyone can hold!"

When a parent's attitude and behavior toward educators and school generally is one of appreciation, optimism, and respect, children tend to adopt the same view. When we demonstrate respectfulness toward teachers, in our words and in our interactions with them, we complete the picture.

> **School-Smart Parenting Tip:**
> **Demonstrate respect for the teaching profession. Let children know that you view education as a life-changing opportunity, worthy of time and effort and, therefore, those who offer it are worthy of respect.**

9. Teach family work by doing chores yourself

According to the U.S. Department of Labor, the typical American household has 37½ hours of domestic chores to take care of each week. Unfortunately, by tradition and default, these chores are largely treated as "women's work." The typical "working Mom" actually has two full-time jobs!

When a family organizes domestic work to provide everyone with equal opportunities and responsibilities, they break down these traditional assumptions. When children see parents actively "pitching in" to take care of what needs to be done, they tend to treat chores as significant. When all members (rather than just the children or Mom, as the case may be) take turns at tasks like doing dishes or washing clothes, a sense of equality and dignity with respect to work develops. When Dad, for example, comes home before Mom and takes care of tasks she usually does, Dad sends a message that he respects and values Mom's contributions enough to take them on himself when it will save her time to be with the family. Not a bad example for children who have the same opportunities!

10. Listen to children

Remember that listening is often an attitude or desire communicated through action. Some self-coaching often helps! For example, one parent we know has a ritual of stopping his car for a moment as he approaches home each day and consciously unpacking his baggage and pre-occupations. He then looks down the street toward home and says, "Regardless of the day I've had, every member of my family has had their own important day! Please, help me be open to what they have to share when I get home!" This essentially breaks the flow of his day and prepares him to effectively listen.

Understand that, while younger children may tell you everything that's going on in their lives, older ones often put up a "No Trespassing" sign. They often keep their thoughts very much to themselves and resent "intrusions." In both cases, listening skills are challenged. In the first, we are challenged to modify our agenda, put down the newspaper, turn off the TV, and give the child undivided attention. In the second, listening skills may be challenged just as much, if not more. How can our listening skills be challenged when the child isn't saying anything? Is the child really not saying anything, or are we not hearing what's being said?

Listening to children often means practicing the restraint of saying nothing and just waiting. Sometimes children don't talk to us because we monopolize the agenda, or invade their space with too many questions: "How was school today?" "Do you have any homework?" "Did you do your chores yet?" Effective listening often results from silence, which allows the child to advance the agenda and tell us what's on her mind. When we follow her agenda and resist the temptation to return to our own, we model effective and respectful listening, the foundation of effective and respectful communication.

11. Let there be love at home

Philosophers throughout the centuries have tried in vain to define love. Books have been written on the meaning of love, the challenge of love, the metaphysics of love, and, of course, the sexuality of love. Each of us has his or her own definition of love. Because love means so many things, our way of showing love may not be interpreted as such by the person(s) we love. Perhaps a simple and somewhat universal definition might be: Love is "a whole lotta like."

When you love others you usually like them "a whole lot," want to be with them yet respect their occasional need to be alone, enjoy their conversation and yet respect their need for quiet, listen to them patiently and offer help when they request it. In short, you treat them "lovingly." In addition to modeling the above behaviors, seek to understand each person and express love in terms that he or she understands. Remember, it is not what we do . . . but how it is perceived!

12. Be spiritual

If love is difficult to define, spirituality is even more so. Paul Tillich, a famous theologian, defined spirituality as "an active sense of identification with things greater than one's self . . . that gives life meaning and purpose." Under this definition, many things spiritual would not necessarily be religious . . . and many things religious would not necessarily be spiritual. However, love, care, friendship, and concern for the poor, the homeless, and the earth, would essentially be spiritual in nature.

What is important here is not a specific faith that we may (or may not) have, but the demonstration that we are committed to something greater than ourselves and that we share this recognition with children. If we are involved with religion it is important for children to observe our participation in any associated rituals and traditions. If we are committed to causes or issues, it is important that we share our passion with children and demonstrate through our behavior that this is a significant part of our lives. For example, we should make our children aware of our commitment to the environment, of our participation in recycling, of the letters we write, of who we support politically and why. This helps them grow to become part of something that adds meaning and purpose to their lives.

> **School-Smart Parenting Tip:**
> Model spirituality by letting your children observe your commitment to issues that give your life meaning and purpose.

Finally, be a model, not a critic. This may best summarize the contents of this chapter. Teach by advocating and doing, rather than through lecturing and critiquing. Kids will learn the importance of doing, acting, and taking necessary steps rather than just talking about issues and principles. By modeling, you enhance their schooling, as well as all aspects of their lives. "Just do it!"

▼

Part

III

The Capable Team

In the next three chapters, we complete our look at developing capable students by encouraging parents and teachers to team up for the sake of children. In chapter 16, we present the "No-Rescue Contract," a vehicle for encouraging dialogue between parent and child, parent and teacher, and child and teacher. The "No-Rescue Contract" in effect asks the question: "What am I willing to let go of so that a child can grow in self-reliance and responsibility?"

In chapter 17, "Networking for Success," we look at the importance of creating a network of supportive individuals. Schools across America are becoming more and more conscious of the need for partnerships and networking. They have responded and are responding with a focus on the family, demonstrated by everything from renewed calls for parental involvement to the sponsoring of formal parenting classes.

In chapter 18, "A Word to Teachers," we close with a word to teachers (but also for parents) in which we offer suggestions for promoting essentially a surrogate family of Contribution, Affirmation, Emotional Stability, and

Modeling in the classroom. Through such strategies, parents and teachers are more likely to be "on the same page" in their efforts to create a supportive environment for capable students.

▼

Chapter

16

The No-Rescue Contract

Mrs. Redbird loved her child so much she could not stand it to push
him out of the nest. In the name of love, her child never learned to fly.
—Positive Discipline Study Guide, *Jane Nelsen*

Before the Pilgrims disembarked from the Mayflower to plant their feet on Plymouth Rock, they wrote up a contract to facilitate and determine the terms of their interactions and governance. The Mayflower Compact, as it came to be called, holds center stage in our history not so much for what it says, but for the precedents it set.

This principle has become an integral part of American culture, namely, to write things down and affix our signatures to them as a sign of commitment. The state constitutions, the Declaration of Independence, the United States Constitution, and the constitutions of dozens of nations that have come into being since our own did and have emulated our need to "write it down," all attest to the power of the signed statement.

The signed statement in the form of a contract is popular in business settings, with the signatures confirming that all parties agree to what has been written down. Many parents have emulated this in parent/child contracts that spell out the rules and consequences regarding such issues as curfews, use of the car, and chores, with both parents and child affixing their signatures to signify commitment to the agreement.

The No-Rescue Contract is designed specifically to encourage effective parenting in school situations. It carries with it a similar degree of seriousness and commitment for the participating parent, child, and school.

What is the No-Rescue Contract? It is a statement, to be signed by the parent(s) and the student, committing both to strive to work together to avoid rescuing and to promote self-reliance and responsibility.

Why a No-Rescue Contract? Because rescuing may very well be the most common barrier we parents erect to our children's developing as capable students. Also a written contract, sealed with our signatures, provides a means through which to attach seriousness to commitments.

Like the mom who rushes to school to deliver a forgotten lunch or the dad who time after time bails his daughter out of some disciplinary situation she has gotten herself into, all parents face the temptation to rescue, probably on a daily basis. The temptation to rescue is a powerful one, presenting itself, as it does, as a test of love. If we love our children, the temptation suggests, we will change our daily schedule to deliver their forgotten lunch, lest they go hungry; if we love them, we will protect them from the logical consequences of their behavior. So goes the temptation.

Shortly after Michael had offered the No-Rescue Contract at his school, a mom complained to him that she did not agree with the idea and therefore she chose not to participate. Michael reminded her that that was fine, that participation in the program was voluntary, that it was meant only as a vehicle through which parents and their children might discuss such ideas as the importance of personal responsibility.

Then Michael asked, just out of curiosity, what exactly in the No-Rescue Contract did she not feel comfortable with. "Well," she replied, "the fact is I *enjoy* being there for my son. I *enjoy* bringing his lunch to school when he forgets it. I *enjoy* dressing him in the morning. I *want* to be there side by side with him if he has problems at school." Who of us can not empathize with a mother's strong desire to provide for her son?

Let's be honest here. Whose needs is this mom focusing on, her son's or her own? Whose needs is she really addressing? What needs of the son are being met by a parent who insists on preventing him from discovering ways to work through life's difficulties? It is so important to remember here that it will never be safer for a child to make mistakes, nor will it ever be easier for a child to learn from those mistakes, than it is in those early elementary school years.

We can allow those mistakes to happen—forgotten lunch, mismatched clothing, forgotten homework—and then, respectfully and supportively work *with* the child to encourage him or her to reach conclusions on how best to avoid the problem next time. By doing so, we will provide a much greater service than when we step in and rescue the child. Asking those simple exploring questions (What happened with your lunch today, Son? What caused you to forget to put it in your backpack? What ideas do you have for helping yourself remember to put it in your backpack tomorrow?) shows far more respect for the child than does continually bailing him out, which only calls into question his progress as a capable person.

> ## School-Smart Parenting Tip:
> **Avoid rescuing. Let children, as much as possible, experience and learn from the results of their actions.**

The No-Rescue Contract was designed to provide the supportive, encouraging framework within which parents and children might discuss the reasons for avoiding rescuing and exploring alternatives to it. We recommend that schools individualize the contract to meet their unique needs, communicate clearly at parent club meetings the purpose of the contract, and encourage parents to sit down with their children to discuss its expectations. If parents choose to participate, they can then sign the contract with the children. (It is often helpful to provide two copies of the contract for each child, one to keep at home and one to return to school to be maintained "on file.")

Central Elementary School
No-Rescue Contract

In recognition of the understanding that our ultimate responsibility as parents is to work ourselves out of the job, and desirous of raising our children as self-reliant young people who will grow to understand that their efforts do have consequences, we hereby pledge to try our best to support them in those efforts by:

Affirming them as capable young people who can dress themselves, do their own homework, pack their own bags, find their own way to their desks, and deal with forgotten homework, supplies, and lunches on their own;

Affirming them as significant young people who are true contributors in our family life, not just objects of our direction or recipients of our rescuing, who can, with our patient assistance, come up with ideas on their own on how best to do their homework, how best to ensure that their clothes are ready in the morning, and how best to remember to bring all their supplies to school; and

Affirming them as young people of influence who can make decisions on their own, experience the consequences of those decisions, and work with us to grow in an understanding of why their particular efforts yielded the results that they experienced.

As parents, we realize that it is far more important that our children make mistakes from which they can learn than that we always look good. We pledge to work with them in both their successes and "near-successes" so that they can learn from them. We understand that just as the teachers do not need to get involved in disciplinary matters that take place at home, we do not need to get involved in disciplinary matters that take place at school.

Teachers do not need to add consequences to at-home infractions, and we parents do not need to add consequences to at-school infractions. We simply need to support each other in our efforts and dialogue with our children to help them gain a greater understanding of what happened, why it happened that way, and what they can do next time to ensure the best possible outcome.

As students, we pledge to do our very best at all times, to take responsibility for our behavior and our assignments, and to work cooperatively with our teachers and fellow students.

And together, we parents and students pledge to treat each other respectfully at all times, understanding that respect is not something that we need to earn but is, rather, owed to every man, woman, and child unconditionally.

Parent Signature(s) _____

Student Signature _____

Date _____

What are the elements of the No-Rescue Contract as illustrated on pages 251–252?

- A heading noting the school's name
- A preamble that clearly states the purpose of the contract, namely, to underscore a desire to provide children with opportunities to grow in self-reliance and personal responsibility
- An affirmation of children as capable, significant young people who can influence what direction their own futures and that of the world in which they will live will take
- A recognition of an appropriate role for parents and of that role's distinction from the role of teacher
- A pledge to be supportive of one another
- A commitment by the young person to take the role of student seriously
- A commitment to mutual respectfulness
- A place for the signatures of parent(s) and child

If your children's school does not yet take advantage of the No-Rescue Contract, bring the idea to the attention of a teacher, administrator, or parent group. Make it a project of your parents' club. Involve teachers and administrators in the formulation of the contract, and encourage participation through education on its merits and clear communication about its purpose.

Have panel discussions involving counselors, teachers, parents, administrators, and (if appropriate) students. Bring in speakers to address the subject. Provide workshops that allow participants to experience alternatives to rescuing, such as allowing natural consequences, fashioning logical consequences, using the what/why/how process, and respecting our children's capabilities. In short, let the No-Rescue Contract become the impetus for a dialogue among all players in the school community—parents, teachers, students, counselors, administrators—a dialogue leading to more capable, responsible, and respectful partners in the education business.

▼

Chapter

17

Networking
for Success

No man is an island,
entire of itself.

—John Donne

Parenting is the most important job you will ever have; it
is also the most challenging and rewarding. To maximize
the potential for success, and to make the job so much
more pleasant, it can help to remember that no person
is an island. Therefore, we do better when we involve
others in the process. Humans are social creatures who
need interaction with others to thrive. We thrive on communication, touch, support, and empathy. We flourish
when we have others with whom we can celebrate tri-
umphs and mourn defeats. We are comforted to know
that we are all in the same boat, and we can learn from
each other how to make that boat sail more smoothly.

The need for a support system has become more critical in the world that has emerged during the last fifty years. In 1940, just before World War II, two out of every three American families had a grandparent actively involved in the household. As a result, two out of every three American families had essentially one or more in-house consultants, potential mentors, in-house trainers, and, most importantly, role models who often had time for the kids. Today only two or three out of 100 have such resources.

Further, in 1940 Mom and Dad were complemented by a vast network of aunts and uncles and friends, in addition to Grandma and Granddad, who shared their values and traditions and who were there to support their efforts. Today, due largely to the mobility of our society, such a natural network of friends and relatives is the exception. Our challenge, therefore, is to recognize what we have lost and seek ways to compensate for it. If we do not have traditional support systems for our parenting efforts, creating alternatives is helpful (if not essential). This is why we must proactively seek out opportunities to build networks in our neighborhoods, in our schools, in our places of worship.

An excellent strategy is that of getting acquainted with anyone and everyone in your community. Children tend to make better decisions when they know that their parents "will know!" For example, one common reason teenage girls start drinking is to please a date. Stephen's daughter once told him that, when a young man she was dating was urging her to drink, she said that she would like to . . . but her Dad would "find out" and that would cause problems for her based on her agreements with her father. When the young man asked, "How would he 'find out'?" she replied, "He talks to everyone and someone is sure to tell him!" In the end she became the "designated driver" and got home safely.

Build and Maintain Your Network!

When a child begins to participate in activities (particularly school) and is involved with other children, find out who the other participants are and (at least by telephone) introduce yourself to their parents. Make them part of your "network" and maintain dialogue with them. Talk about goals, hopes, wishes, and challenges for the children. This can pay tremendous dividends!

Treat a child's teachers as part of your "network"! As soon as you know who will be teaching your child, introduce yourself (at least by phone). Talk with them about their hopes, wishes, and goals for the school year. Share your hopes, wishes, and goals for your child with them. Ask them what you can do to support them. Ask for any specific assistance or support that you need. Then, maintain dialogue with them throughout the year! If problems do arise during the year, your child will then have the benefit of adults who know each other working together to resolve issues, rather than strangers trying to work things out in isolation.

Join Parent Training and Support Groups

Affiliating with support groups and involving ourselves in networks provides opportunities to extend our parenting resources. In doing so, we can share our challenges with others, listen with empathy to their struggles, and grow in understanding through the process.

Our experience in conducting classes through the Developing Capable People parenting skills program indicates that parents typically go through specific stages of awareness. Initially, they look for quick answers, something to "fix" a specific problem, tricks that will make children behave right now.

School-Smart Parenting Tip:
Build support systems to create
an "extended family" that can
help in your parenting process.

In the second stage, parents become aware that there are no effective quick fixes and real solutions require patience and commitment to change. Sadly, some parents withdraw from the process once they learn that any honest parenting approach demands more than quick, easy answers. The current child/parent relationship has developed over five, seven, ten, or fifteen years of living together. It will usually take more than a quick fix to improve that relationship.

The third stage is understanding that improvement is ongoing, and committing to the process. Relationships with significant people change, decline, improve, and develop throughout our lives. Indeed, the wonder of relationships is their dynamism, their capacity for endless change, and their continuous growth.

When parents reach this stage, they clearly see the importance of taking the time for sharing with others, becoming part of support groups, and practicing the art of self-renewal. Continuing growth through awareness is now possible.

Jon's Struggle

The following story illustrates the benefits of becoming involved with parent support groups. Jon, married with three children ages two through seven, came to the Developing Capable People program several years ago. From the beginning, Jon made it clear that he wanted no part of this parenting stuff. He had "more important things to do than spend nine weeks listening to a bunch of women" (he was the only male in a group of eleven). He had signed up only because his wife had insisted upon it. She had started the training a year before and really wanted to provide a united front for their children.

Other than making his reluctance to be present known to all other class members, Jon did not participate in the first session. When he came to the second session, he came without a pencil, pen, or his "Participant's Workbook" (a journal that is essential for full participation in the course). He also made a point of noting that he hadn't done the recommended readings from the previous session. Throughout each session, he looked for points he could disagree with to justify his rejection of the entire program. We call this attitude the **"exclusionary exemption."**

When faced with a challenge, many people show the unfortunate tendency to look for flaws, points of disagreements, or slight shades of difference that will "exempt" them from accountability for the principle or concept. In contrast to the "exclusionary exemption" is the **"inclusionary invitation,"** through which people seek points of agreement, convergence, or connectedness that make the principles or concepts relevant to their lives. Clearly, Jon suffered from a bad case of the "exclusionary exemption."

It is important in such situations to avoid challenging the person directly, since it tends to intensify defensiveness and resistance. Challenge is an important step in the development of skills, but, in general, support must precede challenge for it to produce growth. The perception of support takes time and patience when people feel threatened.

Respecting this principle, the leader refused to take the bait Jon continually threw out. Instead, the leader worked hard to affirm Jon's opinions and perceptions and to offer an inclusionary invitation by acknowledging his contributions to the discussion. Further, and more importantly, other participants in the training modeled this for Jon by refusing to encourage his isolation and striving to affirm him.

Interestingly, Jon came to every session and came on time. He was often the first person there. Frequently, he came without his journal or without a pencil or pen, but he always came. When the class discussed the readings suggested during the week, Jon took delight in announcing, yet again, that he didn't have time to do them. This, of course, didn't stop his offering contrary opinions to every point others brought up.

As the classes progressed, the class noticed that Jon gradually became less and less enthusiastic in offering his opposition. As part of the regular opening activities, participants are invited to share any successes and "near-successes" they'd experienced since the last session. During the seventh session opening activities, Jon surprised everyone by announcing that he would like to share his own experiences first. He told how his daughter came up to him while he was watching television, sat down next to him on the couch, and started poking him in the arm. He told the class that he was about to respond in anger for her disruption when something, he didn't know what or why, caused him to stop.

He asked himself why she was poking him and decided to turn off the television and pay attention to her. He then had the longest conversation with his daughter that he had ever had in his life. She spontaneously kissed him when it was time to go do her homework. He immediately reached for his journal to jot down the thoughts that were "flooding through" him just then. Then, in front of everyone, he lowered his head and sobbed.

Needless to say, it was a powerful moment for the group, a moment that cemented the relationships that were forming during the nine-week course. This moment clearly reinforced the awareness for Jon, and for others, that no person is an island. Through building relationships and creating a sense of community, we can grow. Without the challenge and support of the group, Jon may never have questioned the road he was taking. His involvement in the process of learning how to develop more capable young people, reluctant though it was, provided an opening through which other people could enter his life.

They could demonstrate their support for his efforts and empathize with his struggles. This "network" could offer suggestions for improvement, and provide the incentive to stop and question himself at a critical point in his life. Jon has a long way to go, but it is no exaggeration to say that he took a big step that day. The importance of involving other people in the process of raising children cannot be overemphasized. When we join with others, formally in class settings or informally in social settings, we benefit from other's points of view, perceptions, and experiences. We come to see that we are indeed in the same boat, and we do in fact learn from each other how to make that boat sail more smoothly.

An important key to developing capable students is to take the initiative. Check out the school, places of worship, the community businesses, and so on to locate the various resources and parent groups that are available. Many school systems now have parent resource centers, support groups, and even preschool PTAs (in addition to the regular school PTAs) to encourage involvement of parents and provide them opportunities to come together and form communities of support.

Places of worship across the religious spectrum are gaining awareness of the importance of supporting family life. For many religious groups, the common ground of family support is breaking down old barriers between the various religions. Many are offering or sponsoring courses in parenting, support groups, and hosting community programs.

In the workplace, similar trends are emerging. Businesses are discovering that most often employee absences and job stress reflect problems in the home and domestic pressures. Many are responding with "family friendly" policies, programs, and services.

Opportunities to network with other parents are there. We only need to seek them out. By doing so and taking an active part, we not only help ourselves and our children, we inspire others to get involved in the process of growth as well. We benefit, families benefit, the community benefits, and the world benefits. This is as it should be, because no person is an island. A great strength of the human race is our ability to collaborate. Take advantage of it and model it for the next generation!

▼

Chapter

18

A Word to Teachers

"Why not be a teacher? You'd be a fine teacher. Perhaps even a great one."
"And if I was, who would know it?"
"You, your pupils, your friends, God. Not a bad public, that."
— Dialogue between Sir Thomas More and Richard Rich,
from Robert Bolt's *A Man for All Seasons*

Talk to any veteran teacher about how children have changed over the years, and you'll probably get an earful. If that teacher has been around for twenty years or more, you will no doubt hear something like this: "Back when I started teaching, children would mind. If I told them to be quiet for circle time, they would be quiet. If I told them to listen to me, they would listen to me. If I said no, they accepted it. Today, many of them do whatever they want, whenever they want. I don't know if it's television, daycare, affluence, not enough adults in their lives, or what, but kids today definitely behave differently."

And no doubt we have all heard the old timer's lament: "When I got disciplined at school, that was the easy part. The hard part came when I got home. What I got from my dad for misbehavin' in school was, by far, worse than what I got from the teacher. Today, if a teacher punishes a kid, the parents might sue the teacher!" There is probably much more anecdote than actuality in that statement. However, the sentiment remains.

Yes, many kids today behave differently. We've all heard about the so-called list of "most common discipline problems" that plagued teachers in the '50s, as reported on an evening news show several years back. The list included gum-chewing, speaking without raising hands, being late for classes, and the like.

The news report compared that list to top concerns of teachers in the '90s: weapons in school, teacher assault, drug abuse, gang activity, and so on. Whether such a list of concerns was actually drawn up in the '50s has been debated, but that point is irrelevant. Except in specific schools such as the one portrayed in the '50s movie *The Blackboard Jungle,* drugs, sex, and violence in the schools were rarely concerns of American teachers back then; they are very much our concerns today.

Up to this point, we have focused on parents, and how they can provide an environment of contribution, affirmation, emotional stability, and modeling to help ensure their children's success and happiness in school. Now, the questions are for teachers: How can teachers support parents' efforts to provide this type of environment by reinforcing, in their classrooms, the behaviors just discussed? What steps can teachers take to ensure that their students have opportunities to meaningfully contribute to their own education, just as they meaningfully contribute to the welfare of the home? How can teachers show genuine interest in their students' lives, get inside their quality worlds, and affirm them as unique individuals? And, finally, how can teachers provide emotionally stable environments in classrooms—environments where no students will ever feel threatened or suffer loss of dignity?

That's a tall order—even for parents with two or three children that were raised in the same house with the same values, customs, traditions, lifestyles, and prejudices. It's an even taller order for teachers with twenty-five children, all coming from different households, with a wide variety of values, customs, traditions, lifestyles, and prejudices. But that is the challenge: How can teachers mirror, in the classroom, the same behaviors that parents are encouraged to mirror in their homes?

Opportunities to Contribute: The Classroom As a Cooperative Learning Experience

There is no commitment without involvement: If we want students to be committed to their responsibilities, we need to involve them in the decisions that determine those responsibilities. It is essential that we involve them in the processes through which decisions are made about the classroom, through which classroom problems are solved, and through which classroom housekeeping takes place.

The philosophy of a school is clearly reflected in classroom management. An effective classroom is not a pure democracy, in which the majority decides every issue. However, neither should it be a dictatorship, benevolent or otherwise, in which the teacher makes all decisions. A classroom should be a republic in which a contract that reflects the greater good of all is implemented through democratic principles.

In discussing the social climate of a classroom, like that of a home, it helps to think of it as a system characterized by:

- **A set of principles** that stands above all members of the system, students and teachers alike. These might include such things as mutual respect in all interactions; maintenance of a learning atmosphere; insistence that the classroom belongs to all and is the responsibility of all; respect for the teacher as the person ultimately responsible and accountable for the successful working of the system.
- **A set of guidelines** that includes classroom rules and consequences, chores, and responsibilities.
- **Specific processes** for decision making and problem solving, in which members of the system are involved; these might include class meetings, collaborative learning activities, student councils, or advisory groups.

This social climate functions as a republic. It is a system in which certain principles, determined in advance and standing above all else, serve as parameters within which decision making and problem solving can take place. The system is characterized by universal acceptance of the guiding principles, mutual respect for all participants, subsidiarity (the principle stating that the person(s) closest to the problem should first be allowed to solve the problem), and collaboration. This system is much like the democratic system the United States has been working hard to perfect for over 200 years now, with high points and low points along the way.

Such a system is worth modeling for children, in homes and in classrooms. The following specific recommendations regarding classroom responsibilities and homework are designed to teach and support these principles.

- Use class meetings to establish a process within which discussion about classroom responsibilities, housekeeping, conduct, class work, and homework can take place.
- Ensure that each student has some classroom responsibility, at least for some significant part of the school year; this helps communicate to each student his or her importance and the significance of his or her contributions to the group.
- Assign homework on a regular basis; this helps reinforce the habit of doing homework and communicates that homework is an integral part of schooling.
- Refer to homework in a positive and encouraging way rather than in a manner that communicates drudgery. Refer to homework as "opportunities for further enhancement" which, although it doesn't fool your average sixth-grader, does nonetheless communicate its purpose more positively—and perhaps with a touch of humor.
- Allow for differences in intelligences and talents when assigning class work and homework. Design projects and try to assign work that involves as wide a range of intelligences and abilities as possible.
- Avoid assigning homework that requires parent participation. Remember, homework is the student's responsibility, not the parents'. Not all children have access to parents, and parents should not be expected to sit with their children during homework. Teachers need to ensure that they assign homework that the student can do alone. (Like everything in life, there are exceptions to this. A homework assignment that encourages students to ask a parent, or other significant adult, how life was different when they were growing up, for example, could appropriately and effectively involve the parents.)

Showing Real Interest: Looking for Ways to Affirm Each Child

Margie Stevenson attended a fairly expensive private preparatory school with a reputation for building community among the students and providing a top-quality academic education. When her first report card came home, her mother noticed that she was doing quite well: "A's" and "B's" in all subjects except one; she had a "D" in geometry.

The unusually low grade, combined with the fact that Margie had always done well in math, prompted her mother to call the teacher for a conference. After she introduced herself, she asked the teacher whether Margie was perhaps not paying attention in class or not doing her homework, given the low grade on the report card.

The teacher's reply will not soon be forgotten: "I have no idea why she's doing poorly in my class. In fact, I don't even know who Margie Stevenson is! After all, I've got some six courses to teach with well over 100 students, and this is only the first quarter of the school year."

Teaching geometry may very well be a high priority for Margie's teacher, but showing real interest in the students is clearly not. Two months into the school year, this teacher could not even identify one of her students, much less get to know her or show interest in her. Whether this is more a commentary on that teacher or on the state of schools (large class sizes and student populations numbering a thousand or more), we don't know. But it is a sad situation either way, and one we must be prepared to overcome.

Teachers should make every effort to get to know students. They need to know who their students are, what their interests are, what their talents are, and what their special needs are. This is not easy to do in the classroom. The typical American home has two children; the typical classroom has well over twenty, and many teachers have more than one group of students each day. That difference alone makes the challenge daunting. It is, however, essential to make the effort if we are to communicate to students support for their potential.

Much is written today about different learning styles and intelligences. Students are being identified as visual learners or auditory learners, mainstream or special needs, ADHD or "normal." Teachers are being encouraged, and sometimes enjoined, to devise individual learning plans for each child, to make modifications in the curriculum for specially identified students, and to teach to each child's particular sensory strength and intelligence. The sentiment behind all this, the recognition that each child is unique, is a positive one. Whether a teacher can actually individualize the curriculum to meet each child's needs is, however, arguable. In fact, it is arguable whether or not individualizing education is even a good idea. Does the "real world" individualize itself to meet the needs of each adult? Further, education should not only play to each student's strengths, but also strive to challenge their less strong areas.

What teachers *can* be expected to do is become informed about differing learning styles and incorporate as many as possible, and as frequently as possible, throughout the curriculum, for the benefit of all students. Although teachers probably cannot adapt each lesson to each child's unique learning styles, they can create lessons geared toward many styles and offer them in creative ways to all students.

For example, a lesson on the causes of the Civil War might include textbook readings, teacher presentations, storytelling, songs, poetry readings, student presentations, book reports, student-designed projects, a trip to a museum, a live debate, and even physically acting out a major battle. This approach is certainly more likely to reach all the students than an approach that relies on only one or two learning modalities.

Professional standards call for teachers to use as much diversity and creativity as possible in developing each lesson. This maximizes the possibility that each student will learn to his or her full potential. In addition to being sensitive to the many learning styles, teachers can demonstrate real interest in each child in numerous other ways. Following are several specific ways to communicate to each student that he or she counts in the classroom:

- **One-on-One Time**—special time set aside with each student to learn about his or her interests and needs; there may well be no more effective way to demonstrate real interest in students than to meet with each of them individually.
- **Beginning-of-the-Year Interest Inventories**—giving the students opportunities to write down their favorite things, their likes and dislikes, subjects they'd like to learn more about, and so on gives the teacher ideas for special projects and emphases, as well as the opportunity to learn more about the children individually.
- **Student-of-the-Day (Week, etc.)**—giving the students opportunities to take "center stage," if only for a day or week, allows them to share their interests with the class, and allows the class to individually affirm each student.
- **Portfolios**—this welcome addition to student assessment allows the student to participate in her own evaluation by giving examples of things that *she* feels are significant, rather than just what the teacher feels are significant; in addition, portfolios provide an excellent opportunity for one-on-one attention as the student explains portfolio items to the teacher.

- **Personal Notes**—special notes to children on birthdays, special occasions, or for no reason at all communicate to children that they are appreciated and cared for.
- **Cooperative Learning Activities**—even if the teacher does not learn more about each child during cooperative learning activities, the students will; and they will be given the opportunity to demonstrate otherwise untapped abilities such as group problem solving, peer tutoring, resourcefulness, and cooperation (to name just a few).

It has been stated that one of the best predictors of children's success in the classroom is their perception of whether or not the teacher likes them. Teachers who show real interest in their students—in their unique talents, interests, and abilities—help students feel liked and appreciated; and our abilities are always enhanced when we feel liked and appreciated.

Providing Emotional Stability: The Classroom As a Safe Haven

Madeline Hunter is remembered most for her work on the lesson cycle and the various elements that comprise the effective lesson, from stating the objective to closure. Unfortunately, many school districts took her insights to mean that every lesson must contain every element of the classic lesson cycle, even though Hunter clarified that was not the case. Such, often, is the fate of prophets. Disciples sometimes betray them, often unwittingly.

What Hunter made clear is that, although all these elements are important aspects of the effective lesson, they need not be present in *every* lesson. In fact, she declares quite forcefully that an effective teacher reads the situation and chooses those elements of the cycle that are appropriate. That is the art of teaching. Although Hunter emphasizes that everything in teaching is relative and situational, she makes one universal exception critical to providing emotional stability in the classroom: "We must never cause a child to lose dignity."

In the words used, tone of voice, and attitude displayed, teachers communicate to the student that he or she is (or is not) worthy of dignity and respect. Few parents or teachers would, intentionally, use sarcasm or demeaning words and phrases. These have long been discouraged in the classroom. There are, however, many ways this might happen unintentionally. To pick just one example: How long do teachers wait for a child to respond after asking a question? Research has shown that "wait time" is much dependent upon a teacher's perception of the child and his or her ability.

When a child is perceived as being "bright," teachers generally wait longer. When a child is perceived as "not-so-bright," teachers generally move more quickly to another student. This represents failure to preserve the dignity of the less-bright student, failure to show respect for this child's needs and abilities. Teachers must, therefore, be vigilant, even overscrupulous, in their efforts to ensure that every interaction with students preserves their dignity and self-respect. If students learn nothing else at school, let them at least learn that they are people worthy of dignity.

Walking the Talk: Being a Model for the Children

It bears repeating one more time: We cannot change others; we can only change ourselves. In doing so we provide a model, an incentive, an opportunity for others to change. In that spirit, what behaviors can teachers model

that will encourage students to behave in capable, respectful, and responsible ways?

The following chart (**Modeling Effective Classroom
Behaviors**) lists the same twelve behaviors recommended
for parents in the chapter on modeling and suggests ways
to model them in the classroom:

MODELING EFFECTIVE CLASSROOM BEHAVIORS

Student Behaviors Desired	Teacher Behaviors Needed
1. Be on Time for Class	Model the importance of being on time for class by getting to class early and greeting the students as they enter
2. Enjoy Reading	Read to the students; tell them about books that have been read and enjoyed throughout the years; encourage them to talk about their favorite books; make book reports more enjoyable by giving options for format (written, oral, illustrated, performed); display quality works of literature in the classroom
3. Use TV Wisely	Talk about games and activities that were enjoyed before TV was so dominant; avoid using the classroom to talk about the

(continued)

273

(Modeling Effective Classroom Behaviors—continued)

Student Behaviors Desired	Teacher Behaviors Needed
3. Use TV wisely	previous night's TV shows; avoid careless references to "junk" TV shows; occasionally recommend quality specials to demonstrate discriminating use of TV
4. Display Positive Attitudes	Show students that being at the school is an enjoyable experience for you; be "upbeat" about the school; project positive expectations about the school experience and students' progress and possibilities
5. Show Interest in What Is Going on in the School	Talk about the various school activities; highlight them on the bulletin board; invite the students to share their school activities with the class; attend the various school activities
6. Be Problem Solvers	Avoid trying to solve all the students' problems; emphasize problem solving rather than blaming; throw the problems back to the students with statements such as: "I can see how that would be a problem. Why don't we all try to solve it. You all offer possible solutions and I

	will write them on the board, and then we will choose the best"; use class meetings to encourage them to solve problems
7. Behave Respectfully	Consistently treat children with respect; remember: "There is only one absolute in teaching and that is to preserve dignity"; if the temptation arises to respond to a child disrespectfully, model "time out" by putting off the conversation until feelings are less intense
8. Respect Teachers	Model the above behaviors and be supportive of other teachers, and students will respect individual teachers and the teaching profession
9. Participate in Classroom Chores and Responsibilities	Avoid using clean-up time to catch up on lesson plans or other work; instead, model the spirit of cooperation and the dignity of manual work by doing chores with students during clean-up time
10. Listen Effectively	Avoid interrupting; follow the ten-second rule when asking a question (wait ten seconds after asking one

(continued)

(Modeling Effective Classroom Behaviors—continued)

Student Behaviors Desired	Teacher Behaviors Needed
10. Listen Effectively	student a question before going on to another student); reflect back to the student what he has said
11. Develop Healthy Attitudes About Family Life	Tell students positive stories about personal family experiences; avoid negative messages and stereotypes about gender, family types, and so on; demonstrate positive attitudes about family life
12. Develop Spirituality	Appropriately share those issues and causes that give your own life meaning and purpose; communicate respect for the many ways of being spiritual persons; give explanations for actions that communicate a higher power or a natural law (for example, say "because it's the right thing to do" rather than "because I said so")

Clearly, much is expected of educators. After all, there is no higher profession than that which develops the potentials of the future leadership of our world. It is important that parents and teachers hold each other to the highest standards possible in order to develop capable students. We cannot afford to be anything but the very best we can be.

▼

Michael's Postscript

Looking Forward

Never look back; they might be gaining on you.

—Satchel Paige

I have thought often of those students who entered my frame of reference those seven days in April several years back, occasioning a change in my life direction. The mom who left her husband and asked me to keep an eye on her daughter has been back and forth with her spouse several times since then. She appears to be caught up in a codependent relationship, both with her husband and with her daughter, who needs continuous affirmation at school.

The sixteen-year-old who ran away from home eventually dropped out of school, got into difficulties with alcohol, and is now struggling to hold down a job; Teddy, the would-be stalker, has yet to learn effective communication skills and each day becomes more and more alienated from his parents and fellow students; and Joanna, the fourteen-year-old who regularly brought large sums of money to school, is heavily involved in gang activity.

As for the three abuse calls, I have not had any calls regarding those same three children. Although we still get abuse calls from time to time, I have not since received three in a seven-day period. More importantly, opportunities for parents and teachers to review and improve their skills are very much in place in our community. We now have a process for parents experiencing difficulty in their relationships, as well as for those not yet facing significant difficulties, to come together and learn from each other.

Those seven days in April have not been repeated, nothing even close, and I confidently attribute the improvement to the introduction of the Developing Capable People program in our school community. We are more effectively meeting the needs of the Teddys, Joannas, Marias, Richards, and their parents.

Since my introduction to the world of parent support and training several years ago, I have facilitated dozens of Developing Capable People courses. These courses have involved hundreds of parents, including many teachers. Additionally, I have trained hundreds of counselors, teachers, principals, youth ministers, and parent leaders to facilitate the courses themselves in their respective communities. As a result, the programs are presently offered in schools, churches, and community centers throughout the Dallas area and beyond, reaching thousands more. Facilitators all over the country, indeed in many parts of the world, are doing the same. The world is being changed, one person at a time.

On a more personal note, I have been reconfirmed in my role as educator and school principal. There are still moments of despair (especially during April!), but I now have a response to that despair. I can fall back on my many experiences working with parents, providing opportunities for them to positively change their lives, learning from them so I too can change my own life in positive ways. I now have a process for change, which is a liberating and empowering feeling.

By reading this book, you are part of that change, that process of reviewing and improving your own skills. You have reflected on the stories presented, applied them to your own lives, and, no doubt, made mental notes of changes you would like to make in the future. I close this book by inviting you to jot down those thoughts, thereby formalizing your commitments by putting them in writing. Accordingly, I ask you to reflect now on the possibilities suggested.

What have you identified that you would like to do differently? What specific changes do you wish to make? What behaviors would you like to more effectively model for your children? How, specifically, will you accomplish these changes? Write down your thoughts on the "My Personal Commitment" page that follows. Commit yourself to them. Make them your own. Confirm your commitment with your signature.

It has been said that the healing of a nation begins in the homes of its citizens. I would add that the healing of our schools also begins in our homes. Let's support that healing for our children, and for future generations, by striving to provide an environment characterized by contribution, affirmation, emotional stability, and modeling. By doing so we develop young people who perceive themselves as capable, significant, influential people; who have the self-discipline, interpersonal skills, responsibility, and judgment to live and learn effectively in a constantly changing and challenging world!

MY PERSONAL COMMITMENT

In order to maximize the potential for my children to become capable students, I will make the following specific changes in my life:

Contribution: Organizing My Family to Affirm Contributions.

I will_____

_____

_____

_____

_____

_____

_____

_____

_____

Affirmation: Showing Real Interest in My Children's Worlds.

I will_____

_____

_____

_____

_____

_____

_____

_____

_____

Emotional Stability: Providing a
Safe Oasis at Home.

I will_____

_____

_____

_____

_____

_____

_____

_____

_____

Modeling: Walking the Talk.

I will_____

_____

_____

_____

_____

_____

_____

_____

_____   _____
(Signature)   (Date)

Recommended Reading

Arent, R. P. *Parenting Children in Unstable Times: Your Guide to Workable and Optimistic Parenting Skills to Develop Your Children's Stability and Family Well-Being.* Golden, CO: Fulerum Publishing, 1993.

Armstrong, T. *Multiple Intelligences in the Classroom.* Alexandria, VA: Association for Supervision and Curriculum Development, 1994.

Bedley, G. *Climate Creators: Dynamic Principles for Promoting Positive Self-Esteem in the Workplace.* (1992) Irvine, CA: People-Wise Publications, 1982.

Benson, P. L. *The Troubled Journey: A Portrait of 6th–12th Grade Youth.* Minneapolis, MN: Search Institute, 1990.

Bibby, R. W. and Posterske, D. C. *Teen Trends: A Nation in Motion.* Toronto, Ontario: Stoddard Publishing, 1992.

Bilodeau, I. *The Anger Workbook.* Minneapolis, MN: Compcare Publications, 1992.

Bradshaw, J. *Bradshaw on the Family: A Revolutionary Way of Self Discovery.* Deerfield Beach, FL: Health Communications, 1998.

Branden, N. *The Power of Self-Esteem.* Deerfield Beach, FL: Health Communications, 1992.

Branden, N. *The Six Pillars of Self-Esteem.* New York, NY: Bantam Books, 1994.

Brendtro, I. K., Brokenleg, M., and Van Boerkern, S. *Reclaiming Youth At Risk: Our Hope for the Future.* Bloomington, IN: National Education Service, 1990.

Briggs, D. C. *Your Child's Self-Esteem: Step-By-Step Guidelines for Raising Responsible, Productive, Happy Children.* Garden City, NY: Doubleday & Co., 1970.

Buzan, T. *Use Both Sides of Your Brain, Third Edition.* New York, NY: Penguin Books, 1991.

Clemes, H. and Bean, R. *How To Raise Children's Self-Esteem.* Los Angeles, CA: Price Stern Sloan, 1990.

Clemes, H. and Bean, R. (1981). *Self-Esteem: The Key to Your Child's Well-Being.* Toronto, Ontario: Academic Press, 1981.

Connor, D. R. *Managing At the Speed of Change: How Resilient Managers Succeed and Prosper Where Others Fail.* New York, NY: Random House, 1992.

Conway, J. F. *The Canadian Family in Crisis.* Toronto, Ontario: James Loriner and Co. Ltd., 1993.

Coopersmith, S. *The Antecedents of Self-Esteem.* San Francisco, CA: Freeman Press, 1981.

Covey, S. R. *People Centered Leadership.* New York, NY: Summit Books, 1990.

Covey, S. R. *The Seven Habits of Highly Effective People.* New York, NY: Simon and Schuster Inc., 1989.

Covey, S. R., Merrill, A. R., and Merrill, R. R. *First Things First*. New York, NY: Simon and Schuster, 1994.

Dinkmeyer, D. and Losconcy, L. E. *The Encouragement Book: Becoming a Positive Person*. New York, NY: Prentice Hall Press, 1980.

Dreijurs, Rudolpf, et al. *Children: The Challenge*. New York, NY: E. P. Dutton, 1987.

Dryden, G. and Vos, J. *The Learning Revolution*. Winnipeg, Manitoba: Skills of Learning Publications, 1994.

Dyer, W. W. *What Do You Really Want For Your Children? How To Raise Happy Kids*. New York, NY: Hearst Corporation, 1985.

Elkind, D. *The Hurried Child: Growing Up Too Fast Too Soon*. New York, NY: Addison Wesley, 1988.

Ellis, A. *How to Raise an Emotionally Healthy, Happy Child*. Hamilton, Ontario: Borden Publishing Co., 1980.

Eyre, L. and Eyre, R. *Teaching Your Children Values*. New York, NY: R.M. Eyre and Associates, 1993.

Faber, A., and Malzlish, E. (1980). *How To Talk So Kids Will Listen: And Listen so Kids Will Talk*. New York, NY: Avon Books, 1980.

Fine, M. F., and Carlson, C. *The Handbook of Family-School Intervention: A Systems Perspective*. Needham Heights, MA: Simon and Schuster, 1992.

Gardner, H. *Frames of Mind: The Theory of Multiple Intellegences*. New York, NY: Basic Books, 1993.

Ginsberg, S. and Opper, H. *Piaget's Theory of Intellectual Development*. Englewood Cliffs, NJ: Prentice Hall, Inc., 1989.

Glasser, W. *Control Theory in The Classroom*. New York, NY: Harper & Row, 1996.

Glasser, W. *The Quality School: Managing Students Without Coercion*. New York, NY: Harper & Row, 1990.

Glasser, William. *The Quality School*. New York, NY: Harper Collins, 1992.

Glenn, H. Stephen. *Raising Self-Reliant Children in a Self-Indulgent World*. Rocklin, CA: Prima Publishing, 1988.

Godfrey, Neale S. and Edwards, Carolina. *Money Doesn't Grow on Trees*. New York, NY: Simon and Schuster, 1994.

Goleman, D. *Emotional Intelligence*. New York, NY: Bantam Books, 1995.

Hart, L. *The Winning Family: Increasing Self-Esteem in Your Children and Yourself*. Oakland, CA: Lifeskills Press, 1990.

Healy, J. M. *Endangered Minds: Why Children Don't Think and What We Can Do About It*. New York, NY: Simon and Schuster, 1990.

Helmstetter, S. *Predictive Parenting: What to Say When You Talk to Your Kids*. New York, NY: Simon and Schuster, 1989.

Israel, L. and Buzan, T. *Brain Power for Kids: How to Become an Instant Genius*. Miami, FL: Brain Power for Kids Inc., 1991.

Jenson, E. *Brain Based Learning and Teaching*. Delmar, CA: Turning Point Publishing, 1995.

Jewett, C. L. *Helping Children Cope With Separation and Loss*. Boston, MA: Harvard Common Press, 1982.

Kohn, Alfie. *Punished by Rewards*. New York, NY: Houghton Mifflin, 1993.

Lazear, David. *Seven Ways of Knowing*. Palatine, IL: IRI Skylight Publishing, 1991.

Leman, Kevin. *The Birth Order Book*. New York, NY: Dell Publishing, 1984.

Lickona, T. *Educating for Character: How Our Schools Can Teach Respect and Responsibility.* New York, NY: Bantam Books, 1991.

Main, F. *Perfect Parenting and Other Myths.* Minneapolis, MN: Compcare Publishers, 1986.

Mathews, Jay. *Escalante: The Best Teacher in America.* New York, NY: Henry Holt and Company, 1988.

McKay, M., Davis, M., and Fanning, P. *Messages: The Communication Skills Book.* Oakland, CA: New Harbinger Publications, 1983.

McKay, M., Davis, M., and Fanning, P. *Stop Letting Your Life Lead You! Master Your Own Destiny Through Self-Esteem.* Oakland, CA: New Harbinger Publications, 1987.

McWilliams, P. *Life 101: Everything We Wish We Had Learned About Life in School But Didn't.* Los Angeles, CA: Prelude Press, 1990.

McWilliams, P. *You Can't Afford the Luxury of Negative Thought: A Book For People With Any Life-Threatening Illness—Including Life.* Los Angeles, CA: Prelude Press, 1988.

Mecca, A. M., Smelser, N.J., and Vasconcellos, J. *The Social Importance of Self-Esteem.* Berkeley, CA: University Press, 1989.

Meichenbaum, D. *Stress Inoculation Training.* New York, NY: Pergamon Press, 1985.

Minden, H. A. *Two Hugs for Survival.* Toronto, Ontario: McClelland & Stewart LTD., 1982.

Mitchell, W. *The Power of Positive Students.* New York, NY: Bantam Books, 1985.

Naisbitt, J. and Aburdene, P. *Megatrends 2000: Ten New Directions for the 1990's.* New York, NY: William Morrow and Co., 1990.

Nelsen, J. *Positive Discipline: A Warm, Practical, Step-by-Step Sourcebook for Parents and Teachers.* New York, NY: Ballantine Books, 1988.

Nelsen, J. *Understanding Second Edition, Revised: Eliminating Stress and Finding Serenity in Life and Relationships.* Rocklin, CA: Prima Publishing, 1996.

Nelsen, J. and Lott, L. *Positive Discipline for Teenagers.* Rocklin, CA: Prima Publishing, 1994.

Nelsen, J., Lott, L., and Glenn, H. S. *Positive Discipline A–Z: 1001 Solutions to Everyday Parenting Problems.* Rocklin, CA: Prima Publishing, 1993.

Nelsen, J., Lott, L., and Glenn, H. S. *Positive Discipline in the Classroom, Revised and Expanded Second Edition.* Rocklin, CA: Prima Publishing, 1997.

Ogden, F. *The Last Book You'll Ever Read: And Other Lessons From the Future.* Toronto, Ontario: Macfarlane Walter & Ross, 1993.

Peck, M. S. *The Road Less Traveled: A New Psychology of Love, Traditional Values and Spiritual Growth.* New York, NY: Simon and Schuster, 1978.

Peters, Thomas J. and Waterman, Jr., Robert H. *In Search of Excellence.* New York, NY: Harper & Row, 1982.

Phillips, G. *Home-School Conspiracy: How To Improve Your Child's School Performance.* Vancouver, BC: EduServ Inc., 1992.

Piaget, J. *The Child's Conception of the World: A 20th Century Classic of Child Psychology.* Savage, MD: Rowan and Littefield Publishers, 1951.

Reasoner, R. W. *Building Self-Esteem in the Elementary Schools: Teacher's Manual.* Palo Alto, CA: Consulting Psychologists Press Inc., 1992.

Reasoner, R. W. and Dusa, G. *Building Self-Esteem in the Secondary Schools: Teacher's Manual.* Palo Alto, CA: Consulting Psychologists Press Inc., 1992.

Robbins, A. *Awaken the Giant Within: How to Take Immediate Control of Your Mental, Emotional, Physical and Financial Destiny.* New York, NY: Summit Books, 1991.

Satir, V. *Peoplemaking.* Palo Alto, CA: Science and Behavior Books, 1972.

Schulman, M. and Mekler, E. *Bringing Up a Moral Child: A New Approach for Teaching Your Child to Be Kind, Just, and Responsible.* New York, NY: Doubleday Dell, 1985.

Seligman, M.E.P. *Learned Optimism: How to Change Your Mind and Your Life.* New York, NY: Alfred A. Knopf Inc., 1990.

Thompson, C. I. and Rudolph, L. B. *Counseling Children.* Pacific Grove, CA: Brooks-Cole Publishing, 1992.

Toward a State of Esteem. The Final Report of the California Task Force to Promote Self-Esteem and Personal and Social Responsibility. Sacramento, CA: California State Department of Education's Bureau of Publications, 1990.

Tracy, B. *Maximum Achievement: The Proven System of Strategies and Skills That Will Unlock Your Hidden Powers to Succeed.* New York, NY: Simon and Schuster, 1993.

Vernon, A. and Al-Mabuk, R. H. *What Growing Up is All About.* Champaign, IL: Research Press, 1995.

Index

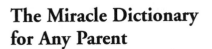

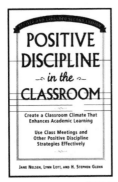